Anderson

D0048224

Growing Compassionate Kids

Helping
Kids See
Beyond Their
Backyard

JAN JOHNSON

UPPER ROOM BOOKS®

GROWING COMPASSIONATE KIDS
Helping Kids See Beyond Their Backyard

The Upper Room® Web site: http://www.upperroom.org

UPPER ROOM®, UPPER ROOM BOOKS® and design logos are trademarks owned by The Upper Room®, Nashville, Tennessee. All rights reserved.

Cover & book design: John R. Robinson
Cover photo credits:
    Girl with baby: © Christopher Bissell/Stone
    Young boy: © Dave Nagel/Stone
    Girl with wagon: © Jim Cummins/FPG International/LLC
    Teens painting: © Ken Chernus/FPG International LLC
First printing: 2001

Library of Congress Cataloging-in-Publication Data

Johnson, Jan, 1952–
    Growing compassionate kids / by Jan L. Johnson.
      p.cm.
    Includes bibliographical references.
    ISBN 0-8358-0932-3
    1. Child rearing—Religious aspects—Christianity. 2. Caring. 3. Helping behavior in
    children. I. Title.

HQ769.3 .J64 2001
649'.1—dc21

00-0043530

Printed in the United States of America

This book is for my tenderhearted daughter
and my strong son,
Janae Johnson and Jeff Johnson,
the two people who continue to teach me about compassion.

Contents

Acknowledgments   ix

Suggestions for Using This Book   xi

IDEAS TO GET YOU THINKING

CHAPTER ONE   Dreaming for Our Children   3

CHAPTER TWO   Moving Beyond My Backyard   13

CHAPTER THREE   Being the Hands and Feet of Christ   23

CHAPTER FOUR   The Key Ingredient of Compassion   35

CHAPTER FIVE   From Self-Protective to Proactive   45

IDEAS TO GET YOU STARTED

CHAPTER SIX   Conversations within the Natural Course of Family Life   57

CHAPTER SEVEN   Making the News Meaningful   65

CHAPTER EIGHT   Seeing Your Community with Open Eyes   73

CHAPTER NINE   World-Class Leisure and Entertainment   81

CHAPTER TEN   Giving Voice to Empathy   87

CHAPTER ELEVEN   Volunteering as a Family   93

CHAPTER TWELVE   Firsthand Cross-Cultural Experiences   101

CHAPTER THIRTEEN   Side by Side with the Church Community   109

CHAPTER FOURTEEN   Linking with a Child Overseas   117

CHAPTER FIFTEEN   Shedding Stereotypes   125

CHAPTER SIXTEEN   Handling Affluence   133

CHAPTER SEVENTEEN   What You Can Expect to Happen   141

Notes   148

Resources   152

Acknowledgments

A lthough I have felt strongly about this topic for many years, the idea for a book took fire and would not die after I wrote an article of the same title for *World Vision* magazine. While doing research for that article, I met many of the people I interviewed again for this book. First, I happened upon Todd and Marge Evans and Elaine Smythe and her daughter Helen. Then I met up with the folks at the Parenting for Peace and Justice Network, including Jim and Kathleen McGinnis; Ken and Gretchen Lovingood and their daughter Jennifer Guevera; and eventually Susan, Jim, and Heidi Vogt.

Also while writing that article, I met another set of parents who cared about these issues and inspired me to do more with my children. They were all affiliated with the Mennonite Central Committee: Earl and Pat Martin, Rachel Miller, Gerald and Sara Wenger Shenk, Marc and Anita Hostetler, and Michael and Virginia Hostetler.

Shortly after that, I was privileged to travel as a journalist with Compassion International to the Dominican Republic to research an article for *Christian Parenting Today.* There I interviewed David and Rebecca Nielson and their two children, Amanda and Wesley, as they met their sponsored children.

By this time, I was aflame with the idea of writing this book, but no publisher seemed to think the topic was marketable. Then I met former Upper Room Books publisher Janice Grana and current acquisition editor JoAnn Miller, both of whom truly heard my passion and validated that this book had to be written.

As time passed, I began interviewing my friends Sharon Norris, Christine Sine, and Barbara Hibschman, and found new friends in Blanca Castro, Kevin Johnson, and Mary and Laura Price. I also had fun reconnecting with others I'd interviewed years before: Jan McDougall of Union Rescue Mission; Jeff Wright of the Center for Anabaptist Leadership; and Jack and Elizabeth Shepherd, who had walked across America reaching out to the homeless.

ACKNOWLEDGMENTS

Most of the people named above are more qualified to write this book than I, so I am grateful for their sharing what they know with this journalist and allowing me to share their insights here.

Over the years folks at organizations such as World Vision, Compassion International, Evangelicals for Social Action, the U.S. Center for World Mission, Union Rescue Mission of Los Angeles, and the Samaritan Center in Simi Valley have faithfully reminded me of Jesus' passion. Perhaps most formative of all, the magazine *Weavings* has shown me issue by issue for fifteen years that inward spirituality results in outward compassion for others.

The stars of the show have been the children we've sponsored and the clients at the Samaritan Center where I volunteer and where my family sometimes joined me. My husband, Greg, and my almost-adult children, Jeff and Janae, have cooperated with Mom's wild ideas and have proven at times to have a much more generous heart than I. Working alongside them has meant everything to me.

Suggestions for Using This Book

Discussion Classes

In addition to reading and enjoying this book, you may wish to form a class that discusses it together. If so, questions are provided at the end of the chapters. Since chapters 1–5 are longer and more explanatory while the rest are short and practical, the following formats would work well for ten sessions and for six sessions.

Ten Sessions

Session 1:   Read chapter 1 and discuss the questions at the end.

Session 2:   Read chapter 2 and discuss the questions at the end.

Session 3:   Read chapter 3 and discuss the questions at the end.

Session 4:   Read chapter 4 and discuss the questions at the end.

Session 5:   Read chapter 5 and discuss the questions at the end.

Session 6:   Read chapters 6, 7, and 8 and discuss the questions at the end. (There are fewer questions.)

Session 7:   Read chapters 9, 10, and 11 and discuss the questions at the end of each chapter.

Session 8:   Read chapters 12, 13, and 14 and discuss the questions at the end of each chapter.

Session 9:   Read chapters 15, 16, and 17 and discuss the questions at the end of each chapter.

Session 10:   Do a group project together with kids.

At session 6, begin to discuss a group project in which all attendees could participate and bring children, grandchildren, nieces, nephews, or friends' children with them. You will probably get more ideas as you work through the practical chapters. Let this time together become Session 10.

Six Sessions

Session 1:   Read chapters 1 and 2 and discuss the questions at the end. Begin discussing the group project.

Session 2:   Read chapters 3 and 4 and discuss the questions at the end of each chapter.

Session 3:   Read chapters 5 and 6 and discuss the questions at the end of each chapter.

Session 4:   Read chapters 7–11 and discuss the questions at the end of each chapter.

Session 5:   Read chapters 12–17 and discuss the questions at the end of each chapter.

Session 6:   Do a group project together with kids.

Personal Devotions

Each chapter includes an outline for this personal time to help you process the ideas and let God speak to you.

Family Devotions

For every session in the ten outlined above, a short scripture verse, a prayer, and possibly a question are provided as a means to share your journey with the people you love. Then, after you've finished the book, they won't be too surprised if you want to take them on a mission trip to Brazil or spend an afternoon at the shelter down the street. They will have seen it coming!

Ideas to Get You Thinking

Dreaming for Our Children

N ow and then in quiet moments, we sit and dream for our children. We wonder how we can help them grow into the people we long for them to be—adults who work hard, who build loving relationships, who know and experience God.

Part of the dreaming picture I have for my children is that God's love will shape them into compassionate people in a culture that is self-absorbed. I long for them to be individuals who like to offer cups of cold water to the thirsty, who dare to whisper words of life to the unreached, who want to love all peoples the way God does, who strive to set aside the pull of materialism and spend their resources on worthwhile purposes.

My efforts to mold them into compassionate individuals are thwarted by the reality of time pressure. Doctor's appointments, soccer games, and homework obligations overwhelm me. To give substance to this dream, I have to be intentional. Over the years, I've met people who have shown me what such deliberate parenting looks like. Here are two stories that illustrate this kind of intentionality.

Elaine Smythe, a homeschooling mom, suggested an unusual idea to her then nine-year-old daughter Helen. Elaine had read about a boy who had a pirate-theme birthday party, but instead of having his friends bring presents, he asked the children to bring the money they would have spent on presents. The boy's family then sent that money to help the family's sponsored child overseas. Elaine asked Helen if she'd like to do a similar thing for their sponsored child, Roberto, in Brazil and let Helen decide.

Helen's birthday party was typical, except that a globe sat on the table along with a letter from Roberto, who was fourteen. The kids held back their "presents" and after the cake, they put the money in a little box. Helen tells how her mom explained that their family prayed for Roberto one day a week. "We told how we wrote letters to him and he wrote to us. I read one of his letters. Then we opened the envelopes and added up the dollars. I thought there would be maybe twenty dollars, but there was seventy dollars! When I look at Roberto's picture now, I think how special he felt when he got the money."

Todd and Marge Evans went out on a limb with their teenage sons. Their sons were used to skiing vacations, but Todd and Marge wanted them to experience a work camp in a developing country. Todd told them they would go back to skiing vacations again, "but just this one time, we were going to Nicaragua to build a school. So my boys and another boy decided to build a basketball court for the kids in the school there. They brought a hoop with them. When the cement was wet, they put their names in it."

Marge—a realistic mom who wanted to prepare her sons—warned the boys that the living conditions there would not be good. "We were right—it wasn't a great big wonderful picnic. We cleared land, made cement, and did masonry work. We saw how people lived with no electricity or phones or televisions but were happy in that setting. The kids respected that even though the Nicaraguans did things differently (like mixing cement by hand), it worked. They were impressed when one of the men used a machete to kill a big snake, so the men let the kids use the machete in their work. The boys worked hard—not like at home! They wanted to make a difference."

Did these boys give up on their parents as hopeless killjoys? No, Matt Evans went back to Nicaragua a second time and later spent seven weeks in Chile with the American Field Service. When he had to write about the experience that meant the most to him for his college application, he wrote about the trip to Nicaragua.

In both instances, these parents were intentional about teaching their children to be compassionate toward the world, but they still had fun. Teaching our kids to be compassionate isn't a matter of sacrificing to the point of being bleak. It's about doing things families normally do (as you'll see in later chapters) but doing them in a way that involves loving others in the world.

Through this book, I hope to strengthen your intentionality as mine was strengthened several years ago when I volunteered for a week at the U.S. Center for World Mission. Daily I saw the needs of people from other countries: needs to hear about God and the gospel; needs to experience justice in unfair situations; needs for food, clothing, and health care. As the week progressed, my supervisor introduced me to his coworkers as a writer who focused on family issues.

When I was introduced to one of the more passionate people who worked there, he came out from behind the desk and grilled me, "Why are parents working so hard to help their kids get good grades, do well in sports, and be involved in youth group? These activities are OK, but do they make a difference? What is the point—to make them sharper, smarter kids? What are you focusing on your family for? Is having a happy, intact family the goal or a means to an end—advancing knowledge of God's mercy and justice on earth?"

Teaching kids to care for people beyond their backyard is one more way to teach our children to love God.

The man's passion shocked me. I excused myself, dismissing him as a missions fanatic who must have had too much coffee that day. Back at my desk, my eyes wandered to a brochure that spoke more gently but just as clearly as my coworker.

Think over the energy you're throwing into life now—trying to be the best you can be, trying to get ahead, to be a better family member, a better you. Why work so hard? Why ask so often for God's blessing on your life?

If it's to have a nicer, happier life that's not a bad goal. Especially since that's what heaven will be—an easier, nicer existence. If that were God's purpose for you right now, [God] would simply take you home to heaven, right? But here-and-now, biblical discipleship is never described as "nice" or "easy."

Go ahead: Break out of the idea that to join God's family is to become part of a nice, privileged group. It's more like being born into a *family business*—everybody is naturally expected to take part in the [parents'] work.[1] [my italics]

As I drove home that day, I wondered what being a part of the "family business" meant to me as a Christian, as a journalist, as a mom. In the quiet of this commute, I began to dream. I was teaching my kids what was important by what I emphasized most—studying hard in school, participating in sports, going to church. These were all fine pursuits, but wasn't my real goal for them to know the heart of God? to join God in important worldwide purposes here on earth? Based on the things I reminded my children about most, the important items in life were being on time, getting homework done, picking up bathroom towels.

I was teaching my children to pray, but service is a spiritual discipline just as prayer is. Service forms us spiritually, teaching us to trust God. As we serve alongside others, we (including kids) can't help asking ourselves: Will God work through the people in charge? (Sometimes you wonder!) Is my small contribution valuable? Will God use what I'm doing even though I don't see the results?

We tend to think of spiritual disciplines as quiet, devotional moments, but Jesus and the disciples not only prayed together; they also worked hard together. A spiritual discipline has been defined as anything that helps us practice "how to become attentive to that small voice and willing to respond when we hear it."[2] If we're going to be cooperative at all while serving others, we'll need to be attentive to God's voice. We can help our children do this by asking them, as we serve together: What does the person I'm serving really need? How can I be helpful to the people I'm working with? How does it feel to cooperate with God and be a part of the "family business"?

Service also teaches us that prayer and work blend together. You may have prayed to love an elderly person, but when you enter a convalescent home and wrinkle your nose at the smell, you get to pray and explain to the children in your life, "I'm praying the odor won't bother us and we'll just enjoy ourselves." We weave prayer with service, the practical feet on the body of Christ.

As the commuter traffic slowed, my mind raced with difficult questions for God:

- How could I impress upon my children that being the hands and feet of Jesus Christ was as important as punctuality, homework, and neatness?
- By encouraging intellectual pursuits and neglecting of character-building activities, wasn't I teaching simple arrogance?
- If my children had good character without a heart for God, wouldn't they be unbearably self-righteous?

Responding to these questions became a journey for me as well as for my family. To my surprise, this effort was not only fun, but I saw it make a difference in their personalities, in our neighborhood, and (by faith) in the world.

CHAPTER ONE

The Yes, but . . . Questions

Maybe you're thinking, Who am I to teach my children or grand-children about loving the world? I am so inadequate myself. I had those thoughts in the car that day. I knew from experience, though, how making other spiritual disciplines, such as prayer and worship, simple enough for my kids to understand had enriched my own capacity for prayer and worship. I decided to do the same thing with service—learn for myself while teaching my children.

Perhaps we can be inspired by teens. They are in a developmental stage laced with a fear of inadequacy, yet they still get involved. A Gallup poll found that "61 percent of American teenagers were volunteering on a weekly basis, compared to 51 percent of American adults. The contribution made by these teenagers was valued at more than seven billion dollars!"[3]

The task is too big, you may think. That's true. Our challenge is to teach children to be *process-oriented* not *product-oriented*. "Mother Teresa was once asked why she kept caring for the sick when she knew that no matter what she did, they would still die. Mother Teresa said, 'Whether they live or die is irrelevant to the act of love.'"[4] She understood that the point of charity is to do the deed in love, not to worry about whether it looks successful to others.

You never know what good can come of an insignificant act. Barbara Hibschman, who served with her family as a missionary in the Philippines for a few years, tells how children in U.S. churches would pack up used clothing and send it to them. "We had a boy in a Christmas program whose parents were poor and couldn't afford the uniform for the program—a specific blue and white polka-dot shirt. We wondered what we should do. Yet three months before, a family had donated [just such] a polka-dot shirt and sent it with other clothes. Two days before the program, the shirt arrived and it fit the boy. It meant a great deal to him and showed him the proof of God's love."

This story illustrates the large truth that we usually don't know the fruits of what we do, which isn't so bad. Not knowing the outcome of our actions enhances the nature of service as a spiritual discipline—we learn to trust God for the results.

Perhaps you have another fear: Teaching children to be intentionally compassionate will get kids worked up about political issues. What I'm suggesting is not necessarily political. I'm talking about behaving like Jesus—caring for the throwaways, making the good news known. The fact that more than 35,000 children die every day of preventable diseases[5] does involve some political issues, but at heart, it's a family issue. Each of those kids has a brokenhearted parent or two. It's a family issue that even though a single famine, earthquake, or flood has never claimed the lives of 250,000 children, malnutrition claims that many every week. An estimated 100 million children live on city streets around the world—with no family, no security, no future.[6]

These may not be my kids, but they're somebody's kids. Being a member of God's "family business" makes their problems my business. As a parent of teenagers with runaway friends living on the streets, I weep when I learn that in Brazil and other poor countries, paramilitary squads are murdering street children in an effort to "clean up the cities."

The church—not the family—should teach kids to care, some will say. Yes, the church should do this job. The school and community should do this job, too. But most of all, I, as a parent, should do this job. Any other influence is trivial in comparison with a parent's. A child's view of the world—including missionary interests, prejudices, stereotypes—is developed largely within the home and extended family.

Won't it scare children to know about desperate conditions beyond their backyard? No, not if presented alongside the goodness of God who *so loves* the world. Christ made his mission clear: "to bring good news to the poor. . . . proclaim release to the captives . . . let the oppressed go free" (Luke 4:18). We're not asking our children to take responsibility for the world's ills but to partner with an all-powerful God in this work.

Concern for people we don't know builds character. As the lack of ethics on Wall Street, in schools, and in politics surfaces, the gospel message stands radically against greed. If we don't intervene, our children will abide by the popular cultural cadence of using people and loving things. The radical message of Jesus is to love people and use things to love those people. Service builds the character of Christ in us.

If we teach children to be compassionate, won't they become soft and vulnerable to exploitation by others? No, not if they practice compassion alongside a wise adult like you and learn what you learn. Then compassionate kids will grow up to be innovative, concerned businesspeople who create good jobs, healthy workplaces, and useful products. They won't cut corners, abuse their workers, or pollute the environment. As union members or politicians, they will be honest and courageous, not greedy and self-absorbed. They will become teachers or church leaders who don't just put in time but have the heart of Christ and invest in the lives of others. They will live life wanting to communicate the heart of God to the hearts of people.

When kids know an oppressed person who was cheated, unjustly evicted, or passed over for a job (and they bear this heartache alongside a compassionate adult like you), they develop the important quality of empathy. When they're included in mission efforts, they become fascinated with people who differ from themselves, and they see the value of Christ's message. This is how they learn the real stuff of life—courage, caring, Christlikeness. They understand that personality, sex appeal, and flair are no substitutes for integrity, consistency, and humility. They learn to admire ordinary people of great character rather than celebrities with great charisma. They see that some things are more important than getting ahead and having more—caring about others, making a way for God's agenda to move forward.

The place for parents and grandparents to begin is with hearts that are touched, not callused. We begin by seeing the people on television news as individuals with real skin that can be bruised, real bones that can be broken, real emotions that can be traumatized, and real minds that can be tortured. This new way of seeing is part

Dreaming for Our Children

of our journey of learning to love God. "How does God's love abide in anyone who has the world's goods and sees a brother or sister in need and yet refuses help?" (1 John 3:17) Teaching kids to care for people beyond their backyard is one more way to teach our children to love God.

QUESTIONS FOR CONSIDERATION

Choose a few of the following questions to discuss with others or to ponder yourself.

1. When and where have your children worked harder than they do at home (as the Evans boys did)?

2. Why do we automatically think that serving with our children might not be fun?

3. How do you feel about the notion of being part of God's "family business"?

4. Which "yes, but" issue below, if any, challenges you most?
   • developing compassion and wisdom while you help the children in your life do so
   • trusting God for the enormity of the task
   • understanding issues that appear to be "political" as family issues
   • presenting the goodness of God alongside the world's needs
   • other

PERSONAL DEVOTIONS

To them God chose to make known how great among the Gentiles are the riches of the glory of this mystery, which is Christ in you, the hope of glory. It is he whom we proclaim, warning everyone and teaching everyone in all wisdom, so that we may present everyone mature in Christ.
—Colossians 1:27-28

CHAPTER ONE

PRAYER. O God, help me to see Christ in my children, "the hope of glory." Show me how I can teach wisdom to them, presenting them mature in Christ. Amen.

FAMILY DEVOTIONS

Read any phrases in this chapter that have spoken to you or that you've underlined—especially phrases that describe your goals for your children. Read these phrases to them.

Reread 1 John 3:17 as quoted in the last paragraph of the chapter.

PRAYER. All-powerful God, show us what it means to dream about being people who _____. Help us to let go of fears about service being boring or scary. Teach us to enjoy working alongside you in your great task of preaching good news to the poor and offering the world's goods to those in need. Amen.

Moving Beyond My Backyard

Our children may be learning about the nations of the world in school, but what do they learn about the world from the adults in their lives? To satisfy my curiosity, I monitored what I read and heard about developing nations for a week. First, I heard some acquaintances discuss vacations, swapping ideas on which beaches in the Caribbean were safe for tourists. Next, I read a newspaper editorial about the adverse effect on America when developing countries fall behind in their World Bank payments. From no source did I hear about the difficult living conditions in those countries. I heard only about ways people in these developing countries could make people in my country more comfortable.

But how could I find fault? I'm not so different from my culture[1] in my obsession with leisure and what is owed to me. I get preoccupied with having the "good life," which leaves me unaware of God's will in the world.

This widespread lack of awareness is ironic, considering we have more world news at our fingertips than ever. We have quit paying attention to overseas news, because it seems so unpleasant. One more natural disaster in a country whose name we can't pronounce is a blip on the screen. That it will take decades for this obscure country to rebuild from this disaster, that a generation of children will not go to school (because the schools are damaged and children are needed to rebuild more essential buildings)—these ramifications escape us. Those of us living in prosperous countries will not know how the rest of the world lives unless we intentionally want to learn. The world may be a global village, but our hearts don't know it.

Also, interest in missions is not what it used to be. Giving people worldwide the opportunity to know Christ has been eliminated from the core of the gospel message. Churches now focus more on how God can solve personal problems. While God certainly does care for us in our troubles, the gospel message is not limited to that.

Let's look at what keeps an online, high-tech, and news-by-satellite nation as unaware of other people's struggles as the "goats" in the judgment scene who asked Christ, "*When* was it that we saw you hungry or thirsty . . . and did not take care of you?" (Matt. 25:44; my italics)

We're disgruntled with things foreign. Perhaps as a result of disillusionment with the Vietnam War, the phrase "southeast Asia" brings to mind casualties, guerillas, and POWs rather than children living today with the consequences of war. These children have lived all their lives on a few square feet of land in a refugee camp after their parents fled the tyranny in Vietnam and Cambodia. In years past, overseas battles were won, and war in faraway places had an aura of gallantry to it. Now, weary of overseas conflicts, Americans talk of getting in, getting out, and coming home. To us, foreign soil is a battlefield, not a home for millions of interesting people.

Increasingly, Americans care more about local matters, because they most affect "quality of life"—an all-consuming concern. Trend observers say we care more about city council votes than national elections, because the traffic signal down the street makes more of a difference to us than federal or international policies.[2] Perhaps subconsciously we think, We take care of our problems; Calcutta can do the same. Unfortunately, Calcutta doesn't have adequate sources of food, much less medicine and construction materials. That reality is unimaginable to Americans living in a country with more grain, technology, and vaccination equipment than it needs.

Moving Beyond My Backyard

I'm protecting my castle. As "quality of life" becomes a consuming concern, we get more picky about who lives near us. Because the needy of the neighborhood "litter" our streets, the NIMBY syndrome has developed: Not In My Back Yard. Homeless shelters and AIDS hospices, among other social service quarters, shut down and search in desperation for places to relocate when the NIMBY syndrome hits.

I recently saw a group of developmentally disabled adults leaving a tiny coffee shop in my mostly residential neighborhood. I laughed, because the location of their group home must be a well-kept secret. Seeing their patient caregivers walk with them turned my heart outward and made my day. I need these "have-nots" in my backyard to help my children and me see compassion at work.

An "us" versus "them" mentality contradicts the hospitality Jesus taught—welcoming into my world the stranger, the hungry, and the imprisoned. "Our culture and the gospel offer us conflicting images of how to use our homes," writes James McGinnis, director of Parenting for Peace and Justice Network. "We speak of our homes as our castles, belying a fortress mentality that infects Christians. We move farther and farther away from people on the edges of our society so we can be safe and comfortable. We build moats around our castles in the form of gated communities and other physical barriers to keep the world out. But Jesus, who had no home of his own, welcomed all and dined with all, especially the fringe people. When we make our hearts and home a harbor for the lost, the lonely, and the poor, we become a household of faith."[3]

We long for quick and easy solutions. "Compassion fatigue" afflicts even concerned people. We feel despair when problems haven't been solved after five or ten years of effort. We're willing to whack away at problems we can fix, but the world's neediness is so big we can't get our arms around it. When I went to the Dominican Republic as a journalist on assignment with Compassion International, I saw many squatter villages where CI funds were making a difference. Several of us on the trip commented on how the American way would be to come in with money, tear everything down, and build everything new. The Dominicans were doing things a step at a time and keeping the community involved. Thankfully, CI leaders in the U.S. were patient with their pace.

What I own, owns me. While growing up in an affluent country is fortunate, it can also teach children to focus on "me." Society's distractions—video games, Barbie dolls, shopping malls—deceive kids; they figure everybody else must live in this privileged situation, surrounded by toys and entertainment After all, don't all the kids in the TV sitcoms live this way? Typically, kids give little thought to those who struggle daily to survive. Even kids' prayers reflect our culture's spirit of acquisition: "God, please help me get good grades. Give me new in-line skates."

If you stand back from the planet to look at who has resources and the ability to acquire them, you'll see that anyone living in a dwelling garage-size or bigger is one of the "rich" of this world (1 Tim. 6:17). Anyone eating a diet better than rice and beans is rich, globally speaking. Two-thirds of the world live mostly on such a diet.

But we don't see ourselves as rich. We gauge whether we're well off by our ability to acquire what is advertised. Jim Wallis of the Sojourners Community wrote, "Advertising is the false spirituality of materialism, promising what it can never deliver. Even the slogans of advertising sound religious, using the language of ultimate concern: 'Buick, Something to Believe In'; 'Miller Beer—It Doesn't Get Any Better Than This'; 'GE, We Bring Good Things to Life.' [This last one is a resurrection image!] Television images of

> *Our job is to help our kids to be God's hands or feet in some way.*

young, beautiful, sexy, successful people enjoying the best of life sur-round almost every product—and you can be just like them, suggest the ads. . . . Is this not the essence of idolatry—a misdirected form of worship?"⁴ Unless you're intentional about the values of God (justice, mercy, and faithfulness), it's easy to become shaped by TV values: You can never be too rich, too thin, or own too flashy a car.

As a globally affluent Christian, my task is daunting: "As for those who in the present age are rich, command them not to be haughty, or to set their hopes on the uncertainty of riches, but rather on God who richly provides us with everything for our enjoyment. They are to do good, to be rich in good works, generous, and ready to share, thus stor-ing up for themselves the treasure of a good foundation for the future, so that they may take hold of the life that really is life" (1 Tim. 6:17-19).

To be rich in good works rather than rich in possessions is radical. Sharing with "have-nots" means leaving behind part of my income: "When you reap the harvest of your land, you shall not reap to the very edges of your field, or gather the gleanings of your harvest; you shall leave them for the poor and for the alien: I am the Lord your God" (Lev. 23:22). How did the original hearers react to this injunction? Judith Smith points out, "Not all of those Hebrew landowners were wealthy. They not only had themselves to feed but workers to pay as well. This was their crop, their harvest. They had worked hard for it and they were entitled to all of it. So are we. We are entitled to the money we earn, the food that it buys, the things that make our lives comfortable. What does it mean for us to choose to take less than our entitlement? That is a tough question for us and an even tougher con-cept to teach our children."⁵

Kids, of course, have the added pressure of peers, who squelch compassion by urging them to be cool. Rachel Miller, a mother of two boys, watched her sons deal with this. "Even when other kids are cruel, yours won't want to be different from others. My sons were going to a Mennonite school, and there were some Russian students in Jebb's class. They were different and hardly knew English. Kids referred to them as 'foreigners' and 'Communists.' A lot of kids didn't bother with them, but Jebb was willing to spend time and befriend one of the Russian guys."

It Begins with Me

If I'm to teach compassion to my children, I do, however, have to admit my shortcomings. Here are some of mine.

I'm afraid. While we're concerned by kids' lack of compassion, we also worry when they do want to reach out. I've wondered, Should my small children see television specials about starving children? Is it a good idea to take my teenage daughter with me to volunteer at a drop-in center for the homeless? If one of my kids wants to be a missionary or work with inner-city kids, will I pat her on the head and say, "We'll see," instead of praying, "Lead this child and help me support her"? In trying to be good parents, we isolate children from suffering. While this may be wise in the most extreme cases of massacre or rape, we need to let them see how the rest of the world lives.

In her book *Teaching Your Kids to Care,* Deborah Spaide tells a story about an American woman whose husband was a soldier in Somalia taking food to starving people. When interviewed, she was asked how her children felt about their father's helping. She said she didn't want them watching the news because it would hurt them to know others were starving.

Spaide talked about how this distancing of children from pain doesn't help. It denies that the problem exists. Instead, she suggested that "the mom [could have] allowed her children to see the problem, feel the pain, and find opportunities to help. Perhaps the kids could have started a food drive in school and sent the food to Somalia with the next crew. Or perhaps the kids could have sent 'keep up the good work' cards to the soldiers who were in Somalia."[6] This opportunity would have been ideal, because the children could not only have seen the needs of others but how God uses people to meet their needs.

I'm unaware. My other problem is that I'm so oblivious to how the world lives. From my nice, middle-class neighborhood, God's global causes seem far away. Yes, I care that thirty-five thousand children die every day, but I also care that my carpet has stains. I hear God's call to share my possessions, but I am like the rich young ruler Jesus challenged. I feel bad, but I don't want to live on less.

I recognized this contradiction in myself one day as I was brooding over how the vertical blinds in my living room did not match exactly the paint on my wall. Had I mismatched the colors to begin with? Had the paint faded? The peaceful look of my home now seemed tarnished. As I pondered this, I opened my mail. I sat down to read *Global Prayer Digest* (*see* Resources), which offers daily doses of mission information.

The story that day was about children in Bombay who are captured by traders and sold to wealthy people. Their owners tie them to the bellies of camels during camel races. The children's screams make the camels run faster. Most of the children die from this treatment, although some survive with deformities or brain damage. Operation Moses (a part of Indian National Inland Mission) rescues these kids, breaking into locked Bombay apartments where the children live among rats and cockroaches awaiting their sale. I collapsed on my sofa, praying for these children and for the rescue workers who endanger their own lives to do this work.[7] Most *Global Prayer Digest* readings are not that heart-wrenching, but this one, like many others, pulled my thoughts away from wondering whether I could afford new vertical blinds to perfectly match my walls.

Where to Start

As parents and grandparents, then, our job is to help our kids be God's hands or feet in some way. The great commission is for all, even families: "Go therefore and make disciples of all nations, baptizing them in the name of the Father and of the Son and of the Holy Spirit, and teaching them to obey everything that I have commanded you" (Matt. 28:19-20).

CHAPTER TWO

Where do we begin? Chapters 6 through 17 will give you hands-on
eas for helping the children in your life reach out in compassion to
e world. Before we explore those practical suggestions, though, let's
e a look at how to approach this task. Be aware that it's possible to
very good things with a heart that's out of kilter, and we want to
id that mistake.

As we examine our own thoughts and motives, the next step is to
y. Something like this prayer, used by Bob Pierce, founder of World
ion, is fitting: "Let my heart be broken with the things that break
heart of God."[8] That broken heart moves us to a desire to be the
ds and feet of Christ.

QUESTIONS FOR CONSIDERATION

hoose a few of the following questions to discuss with others or to
der yourself:

Which of the stories about parents in this chapter do you identify with most?
- Rachel Miller's watching her sons reach out to kids regarded
as "different"
- the mother who didn't want her children to see kids in
Somalia starving (or author Deborah Spaide, who suggested
the children should have watched the news and done something to help the children)
- my preoccupation with vertical blinds until I read about the
kids dying in camel races

What has to change inside people to make them willing to welcome "have-nots" into their neighborhood?

Is it difficult for you to overcome preoccupation with having the
"good life" in order to truly care about people overseas? Why or
why not?

Many times people talk about our being "the rich" in this world to produce guilt and get us to care. ("Eat your vegetables. People in India are starving!") How can we talk about our being "the rich" of this world to our children in a way that produces a desire to give?

5. Think for a minute: Has God been speaking to you at all lately about being shaped by TV values (you can never be too rich, too thin, or own too flashy a car)? If so, how?

6. How can you help your children know that service to others is just as important to our spiritual life as praying and reading the Bible? For example, what comments about God or love could you make before or during times you serve together as a family? How might your family pray about service you perform together?

PERSONAL DEVOTIONS

Read the following verse and pray each phrase, using the suggestions as needed.

As for those who in the present age are rich, command them not to be haughty, or to set their hopes on the uncertainty of riches, but rather on God who richly provides us with everything for our enjoyment.

—1 Timothy 6:17

Suggested prayer comments:
- Thank you that you have allowed me to be "rich" in this "present age."
- Show me the ways that I am haughty.
- Forgive me for putting hope in riches and possessions.
- Teach me to rely on you.
- Thank you for supplying so much for my enjoyment.

FAMILY DEVOTIONS

Try adding the following phrase to your mealtime prayers or bedtime prayers. If your children ask you about it, explain it as best you can. If they don't ask, let the explanation wait.

The phrase is, "Let my heart be broken with the things that break the heart of God."

PRAYER. Show me, O God, what breaks your heart, what makes you upset, what you want me to grieve over. Link my heart to yours. Amen.

Being the Hands and Feet of Christ

O ver the years, I've continually gotten bogged down with the minutiae of parenting and let the compassionate emphasis slide. The one thing that brings me back to it over and over is reading and hearing the Gospels.

In the Gospel narratives, I'm constantly fascinated and challenged by Jesus, who proclaimed truth about himself while offering cups of cold water to the throwaways. He crossed barriers without a second thought, seeing only the heart of the person in front of him. He was of one heart with God, the protector of these throwaways. Each time I encounter Christ's radical behavior, I walk away wanting to behave as he did.

Let's take a closer look at how large a portion of the personality of God, the Creator, and Jesus, the Redeemer, involves showing compassion.

God, the Guardian of the Needy

While some people view God as one who favors the good folks and helps those who help themselves, the biblical picture of God is much different. Rather, the passions of God run in these directions:

Mercy to the poor. While most people avoid, stare, or laugh at the bag lady ambling down the street, God tenderly loves the poor, including her: "Father of orphans and protector of widows is God in his holy habitation" (Ps. 68:5). Overlooking the poor isn't acceptable: "Whoever gives to the poor will lack nothing, but one who turns a blind eye will get many a curse" (Prov. 28:27).

God identifies closely with the poor. The way you treat the poor is the way you treat God: "Those who oppress the poor insult their Maker, but those who are kind to the needy honor him" (Prov. 14:31). "If you close your ear to the cry of the poor, you will cry out and not be heard" (Prov. 21:13).

Justice for the oppressed. God commissioned the Israelites to become modern-day public defenders, so to speak, defending the causes of the needy, maintaining their rights and pleading their cases (Prov. 23:10-11; Deut. 27:19; Ps. 82:3; Isa. 1:17). God insisted on fair commerce and business practices (Lev. 19:35-36); God used the year of Jubilee to cancel debt, check slavery, and prevent unfair advantages (Lev. 25:10-54; 27:17-24).

Love for all nations. According to the covenant with Abraham, Israel's purpose was not to be a nation of privilege but a nation through which "all the families of the earth shall be blessed" (Gen. 12:3; 17:7, 13, 19). Israel was chosen to be "a light to the nations" (Isa. 49:6). Throughout the Hebrew Scriptures, God's people helped Gentiles: Elijah helped the widow of Zarephath; Elisha healed Naaman; Daniel worked with Babylonian-Persian kings. God's mission to the Gentiles downright scared Jonah so much that he took off. Nineveh? No way.

These attributes—mercy for the poor, justice for the oppressed, love of all nations—permeate the life of Jesus. When we tell children Bible stories or listen to sermons with them, we can point out these characteristics.

Mercy to the Throwaways

Jesus specialized in the have-nots, the throwaways. He urged the haves to give to the have-nots, telling the ruling Pharisee to quit hosting feasts for friends, relatives, and rich neighbors but to invite "the poor, the crippled, the lame, and the blind," who could not repay him (Luke 14:12-14). He recommended that the rich young ruler give all his money to the poor (Luke 18:22). After talking with Jesus, Zacchaeus promised half his goods to the poor (Luke 19:8).

When Jesus went to preach in his hometown, he scandalized the townspeople not only by claiming to be the messiah but by urging them to reach out to the throwaways:

> The Spirit of the Lord is upon me,
>   because he has anointed me
>   to bring good news to the poor.
> He has sent me to proclaim release to the captives
>   and recovery of sight to the blind,
>   to let the oppressed go free,
> to proclaim the year of the Lord's favor.
> —Luke 4:18-19

Jesus recognized that the have-nots were without voice in that culture; no one paid attention to them or respected them. Of those people who had no "say," Jesus listed several categories in a judgment-scene story (Matt. 25:31-46; italicized below). In our time, who fits into those categories? Here's a start.

- *The hungry and thirsty.* Malnourished people (almost half of the world's population[1]), unemployed and underemployed people in your town, homeless in your town, inner-city and rural poor.

- *Strangers.* Immigrants; new kids on the block; anyone with an accent; street kids; school dropouts; "children who flock to the cities in droves out of abusive homes and divided homes and poor homes and good homes that simply can't handle them; . . . elderly abandoned in old houses with leaking roofs and dirty windows and uncut yards; foreigners who are [viewed with suspicion] just because they do not think or live or look like we do."[2]

- *The sick.* Nursing home residents, anyone with an incurable or chronic disease, the physically disabled and developmentally disabled, those with personality disorders and eating disorders, anyone who can legally park in a handicapped parking place, the herpes-ridden, the HIV positive, AIDS patients, anyone waiting in a trauma center, infertile couples, women with unwanted pregnancies.

- *Prisoners.* Kids serving time in youth facilities; families of prisoners; parolees (many of whom are homeless); those imprisoned by addiction to drugs, alcohol, gambling; Christians who are imprisoned worldwide for their faith (two hundred million Christians suffer massacre, rape, torture, beatings, imprisonment, harassment, and severe discrimination[3]).

Every society has its hierarchy of worthiness. Voiceless people include anyone lower on the cultural ladder than others. They must keep quiet because of their power-down positions in society. Some power-down/power-up relationships we recognize are

- children as opposed to adults;
- women as opposed to men;
- minority races as opposed to majority races;
- poor as opposed to middle class; middle class as opposed to rich;
- lower-paid workers as opposed to highly paid workers;
- less intelligent as opposed to the more intelligent;
- labor as opposed to management;
- blue-collar workers as opposed to professionals.

When voiceless people do speak up, no one takes them seriously because they don't have the status, money, age, or know-how to command respect. Jesus, however, routinely put ordinary, voiceless people in power-up positions. He came to the conversation with the woman at the well with all the power on his side—gender, respectability, ethnicity (not to mention being the messiah). Yet he gave her power by asking for her help.

I first began to understand voicelessness many years ago through my friendship with Edith (not her real name), a homeless woman who walked the streets with a shopping cart. When my preschool kids and I walked with her, people looked right through us. She was voiceless in the sense that no one saw her or heard her. "Our basic sin is one of refusal: a refusal to become interested in others and go out toward them, a refusal to be touched by their distress, to help and sympathize with them. . . . We belong to Christ only by belonging to others."[4]

Jesus' love for all *nations* gave him an inclusive view of life, enabling him to reach across cultural barriers proactively. He taught that all nations should hear the proclamation of repentance and forgiveness (Luke 24:47) and that his disciples—that's us—are to "make disciples

This book isn't about doing compassionate things or social action as much as it's about forming relationships with people. These relationships heal everyone involved.

of all nations" (Matt. 28:19). In the Gospels, Jesus traveled outside Jewish territory and interacted with Gentiles whom an upstanding Jewish teacher shouldn't have been caught dead talking to—a woman of the Samaritan race; a plucky, Syro-Phoenecian woman who came after him pleading for her daughter; a naked, screaming man on the "other side" of the lake (as in the "other side of the tracks").

Love in Action

Respect. Giving a voice to others is about respect. "Suppose a man comes into your meeting wearing a gold ring and fine clothes, and a poor man in shabby clothes also comes in. If you show special attention to the man wearing fine clothes and say, 'Here's a good seat for you,' but say to the poor man, 'You stand there,' or, 'Sit on the floor by my feet,' have you not discriminated among yourselves and become judges with evil thoughts?" (James 2:2-4, NIV).

The natural tendency is to withhold respect from a homeless person, which implies that riches are what make a person. We view the homeless as being in a power-down position because they're lower in the social pecking order.

When I first volunteered at the Samaritan Center, a drop-in center for the homeless, I caught myself being disrespectful in subtle ways: stepping in front of a client or neglecting to say thank you when a client helped. It was as if common courtesy was not necessary with these non-persons. By the time my kids began volunteering with me occasionally, I was able to explain what was happening this way: "How do you feel when all the adults ignore you? That's the way these people are treated most of the time. If nothing else, we're here to notice them."

I cringe now that in the early days of my relationship with Edith, I kept trying to impose my wishes on her. I urged her to attend church with me. I insisted that I should take her to a shelter, even though she liked the streets better. She didn't seem to appreciate my help! I questioned how deserving she was! Finally, I saw that my "charity" wasn't about her but about my need to feel like "a good

Christian." I somehow thought my power-up position in society gave me the right to tell her what to do. Instead of running over her, I needed to listen to her and accept what she said the way I would for any friend.

So one day, sitting on a bench at a bus stop with Edith, I asked her, "What is the most helpful thing I could do for you?"

"Sit here and talk to me," she said. "Nobody talks to me. People look right through me."

Her words were like a whack on the head. Christ did a lot of sitting and talking, in between such other wonderful things such as operating a divine medical clinic and food pantry (feeding five thousand at a time). He respected people and asked them questions. If I can look into someone's eyes and let that person set the agenda for conversation, I place that individual in a power-up position.

Giving with respect means asking people what they need rather than giving whatever is convenient. I get annoyed at people who donate fancy dresses and suits to the Samaritan Center. We make it clear we need socks, underwear, t-shirts, and jeans. Yet I caught myself gathering up well-worn socks and jeans with holes in the knees to donate. I looked at my kids and said, "I think I'd like to give Jesus socks without holes. Let's go buy some."

Solidarity. Of the hungry, the thirsty, the sick and the imprisoned, Jesus said, "Just as you did it to one of the least of these who are members of my family, you did it to me" (Matt. 25:40). He identified with the voiceless, so that their hunger became his hunger and their imprisonment became his imprisonment.

Solidarity is about "suffering with" others—touching someone else's reality, hearing others' stories. So please understand that this book isn't about *doing* compassionate things or social *action* as much as it's about forming relationships with people. These relationships heal everyone involved. Helping the poor melts our isolation and materialism. My world is larger—and so is my kids' world—because of our friendships at the Samaritan Center. We connect with people there. Out of those connections flow desire, hard work, and even sacrifice.

Reciprocity. Compassion doesn't allow power positioning but instead fosters mutual helping. "The poor are more than their poverty. The disabled are more than their disability. The elderly are more than their weakening bodies."⁵ The people we "help" cheer us up. They give us good ideas. They become friends.

I've tried to let my kids see how much I receive from volunteering at the Samaritan Center. They know the Vietnam veteran who gave me the leather key chain I use. They know he probably will never feel comfortable living inside a house again. They see a tiny silver box on my desk given to me by a young woman whom I'd helped many times but became close to only when my father was ill. When he died, she gave me the heart-shaped box and said, "I want you to have this."

Personal care. Jesus didn't "hit and run" with the gospel. He held leprous hands. As we learn to respect those we serve, our help becomes more personal and less institutional.

Involving people we serve in face-to-face, personal conversations gives them a voice. Both the giver and the recipient are helped, because what is most needed by both are healing, caring relationships. A giver needs to see a real face on poverty, and a gift is better appreciated when it has been offered with a face of love.

Here's a good example of personal caring yoked with practical helping. Sharon Norris and her two sons, Matthew and Mark, gathered up clothes the boys couldn't wear and toys they'd outgrown to give to a family in need. "When we took them to the family, the mom and I sat and talked. The kids played together." Why didn't Sharon just drop the stuff on the porch and leave? "If I were in need," Sharon said, "I'd like for the person to be friendly rather than just dropping stuff off. I'd like to meet someone who could identify with me."

The more personal the service, the better. For example, suppose a youth group raises money to feed the homeless at a certain shelter in town. The project becomes more personal when the kids actually collect the food and take it to the shelter. Better yet, they could go to the shelter and make sandwiches there, then leave. Best of all, the kids could make the sandwiches, serve beverages, then sit down and interact with the guests. Jesus acted at that last, most personal level.

Justice for All?

Jesus not only showed mercy; he also looked at the root problems causing people to need so much mercy. He confronted the Pharisees for manipulating people politically and economically (Matt. 23:23; Mark 7:9-13). He continually set an example for us "to loose the bonds of injustice, . . . [and] to let the oppressed go free" (Isa. 58:6). Acts of justice get to the root of why people are disadvantaged in any way and include speaking out about these situations.

What does "doing justice" with kids look like? You may engage the children in your life when you sit down to write a letter to an organization or corporation about their unjust behavior. When you make appropriate phone calls to help someone speak up about a disability claim or to voice concern about the way an institution does business, let your kids see and hear you. Ask them to pray that you'll be calm and firm. You are setting an example as you exhibit the heart of Christ without bitterness or cynicism. Kids need to sense our hope that even if the powers-that-be don't grant our request, God, the guardian of the needy, will meet people's needs somehow.

Children need to learn that when we speak up for justice, it's not out of self-interest. Gretchen Lovingood relates a story about her son, Steve, that illustrates the distinction between speaking out for justice and self-interested complaints. At Steve's high school, flags of different countries were displayed on election day. One of them was a Confederate flag. That bothered Steve. He asked the person in charge if the Confederate flag should be taken down; they had learned in social studies that it didn't represent freedom. Later he noticed that the flag was gone.

"When he told us about this, we applauded him," Gretchen said. "But it just so happened that the staff member in charge was the only nonwhite member of the staff. Since we're African-American, we asked Steve, 'Did you go to her because you thought she would understand?' He said, 'No, I told her because she was the one in charge.'"

Steve didn't ask for the flag to be taken down because he was hurt or mad or because he saw an opportunity for a nonwhite teacher to side with him. He spoke out because he believed it was right for everyone at school. He defended his request with information he'd learned in social studies. When speaking up for justice it's important that the motivation is not personal (what makes *me* feel important) but is centered on what's right according to God's standards.

Salvation or Soup?

Jesus' life reveals that he didn't separate Bible teaching and social issues, as people today often do. Along with words of truth, he offered merciful deeds. The two cannot be separated. "For years, Christians have divided themselves over the most effective means of transforming our world: verbal proclamation of the gospel—witnessing—or social action. . . .Without both, there is simply no Good News. And one thing ties them both together: prayer to a God of temporal justice and eternal salvation."[6] To be the body of Christ in this world is to be the hands and feet of Jesus. Jesus healed both bodies and souls.

Let's say Jesus opened a day-care center in your town. Would he teach the children Bible stories and never feed them (teaching only)? Would he give them snacks and not tell them about God (soup only)? Try to picture it. Wouldn't Jesus teach these little ones to love newcomers (strangers)? to love all nations (racial reconciliation)? to care for creation (responsible environmentalism)? to love those who hate them (nonviolence)? to love people who had done a great deal to be shunned (prisoners)?

This book blends social action and mission into one focus, because Jesus cared for a person's whole being by meeting physical and spiritual needs at the same time (Matt. 9:2-7). He offered a cup of cold water to the body and the cup of salvation to the soul. Both social action and mission begin with prayer, something we parents can teach our kids to do. As we lay them down to sleep, we pray for help in knowing how to feed souls.

QUESTIONS FOR CONSIDERATION

Choose a few of the following questions to discuss with others or to ponder yourself.

1. How do you respond to the idea that the way you treat the poor is the way you treat God? "Those who oppress the poor insult their Maker, but those who are kind to the needy honor him" (Prov. 14:31).

2. Which aspect of God, if any, is most surprising to you?
   - God's tremendous mercy for the poor
   - God's desire for us to treat the poor as we would treat God
   - God's insistence on loving all nations
   - God as defender of the poor and source of justice for the oppressed

3. Reread the lists under the heading "Mercy to the Throwaways." Who would you add to that list?

4. What have you had to learn about respecting a person who is voiceless or about showing reciprocity? How would it feel to tell your children about what you've learned?

5. One important principle of compassionate behavior is, The more personal the service, the better. Why do you think that is?

PERSONAL DEVOTIONS

Read the story of Jesus' interaction with Legion (Luke 8:26-39). How did Christ show him mercy? How did Christ exhibit justice by standing up for him?

PRAYER. O God, teach me to care about people whom others find disgusting. Help me to show them mercy. Help me to stand up for them. Help me to learn something from them. Amen.

FAMILY DEVOTIONS

Whoever is kind to the poor lends to the Lord, and will be repaid in full.
—Proverbs 19:17

PRAYER. We recognize, O God, that you love the poor. You want us to show mercy to them and defend them. Show us how to do that in ways that are respectful. Show us how they can help us. Amen.

The Key Ingredient of Compassion

A s violence on school campuses escalated several years ago, a teachers' magazine asked me to write an article about violence-prevention programs and find out what made them work. As I interviewed teachers and previewed violence-prevention programs, I heard this recurring theme: empathy. Teachers who had spent months teaching kids about doing good instead of doing harm saw that a primary requirement for success was helping kids have a sense of how other people feel.

Helping children become compassionate develops such empathy. As kids connect with God's worldwide purposes, they get in the habit of thinking about other people's feelings. Growing compassionate kids, then, is a powerful antidote to the violence in our culture.

Empathy means putting ourselves in the shoes of another person and identifying with that person's situation and motives. We stop asking, What's in it for me? and How will I benefit? Instead, we look into the hearts of others and share their joys and sorrows. Eventually we understand why they do what they do and may feel a commonality with them.

Empathy is difficult for children, as Virginia Hostetler pointed out to me: "It's even hard for adults, but that's what the gospel is about. Do unto others as you would have them do to you.

Empathy requires imagination." We must ask our kids to imagine how someone feels, how that person hurts, how desperate is that person's need for help.

How Empathetic Adults Are Formed

Shaping a foundation of empathy is difficult, because so many forces are eroding it. Kids who see people killed on television may not consider a starving child's problem as real—it's only on TV. In a culture of hate crimes and subtle prejudice, children isolated from other cultures wonder, How can I relate to that person? She doesn't look like me.

Empathy isn't just a matter of personality (although some children do seem naturally more compassionate). Distinct factors in upbringing can build empathy and compassion in people, writes Doug Huneke, a minister and religious educator. Huneke interviewed three hundred rescuers of Jews during the Holocaust, trying to find out why the rescuers helped or hid Holocaust victims while others stood by. What made these people risk their safety to help others? During these interviews, he looked for qualities or experiences they had in common. He figured that if he could find them, perhaps these things could be taught or nurtured in children to encourage compassionate, risk-taking behavior.

Combining what he found with other studies, Huneke was able to name ten characteristics that rescuers generally had in common. In his book *The Moses of Rovno,* the story of an exceptional rescuer named Fritz Graebe, Huneke describes these ten shared experiences or characteristics.[1]

1. Adventuresome. Rescuers tackled childhood problems and worked toward goals. (Fritz Graebe taught himself to stop stuttering.)
2. Identification with a morally strong parent. (Sometimes this was a grandparent.)
3. An experience of marginalization or being left out or undervalued (such as being in an immigrant family or different in some way).

4. Empathetic imagination. Defined by Huneke as the ability to "place oneself in the actual situation or role of another person and to imagine the effect and the long-term consequences of the situation or the role on that person."[2]
5. Ability to present oneself, speak up, and be persuasive, often through public performance while growing up.
6. Skilled at cooperating and being responsible to promote the well-being of others.
7. Exposed to suffering at an early age.
8. Ability to examine their own prejudices.
9. Belonging to a community or group who valued compassion, so there was not a sense of being in a struggle alone.
10. A home where hospitality was of high value. (Hospitality included the act of taking time to talk to people who needed to talk. Their homes weren't castles to keep the world out.)

The morally strong parents or grandparents with whom rescuers identified (number 2) articulated the importance of compassion, even though it made them unpopular. Fritz Graebe said, "My mother always urged me to do what I—I, not others—thought was best and right."[3] One of the things his mother did, which developed his empathetic imagination, was to ask him "regularly and in many different situations, 'And Fritz, what would you do?'" His mother insisted on visiting an imprisoned relative in spite of "intense family pressure and parental abuse." When Fritz asked her why, she responded with a brief explanation of her own concerns and that question, "And Fritz, what would you do?"[4]

Several of the characteristics above indicate that rescuers were influenced by empathetic family members. Exhibiting a hospitality of the heart, parents or grandparents gave an ear to the hurting, and they invited people into their lives. Even though rescuers had experienced marginalization as children, their constructive parents turned that into something positive instead of allowing the children to become bitter.

More clues for building empathy in children are provided by the Search Institute, a leading researcher in the formation of positive values in adolescents. "There are two primary sources [for caring values]," writes Peter Benson, in *All Kids Are Our Kids.* "First, caring, like all values, is passed on by *modeling.* It is rooted in the experience of being with people who choose to respond to human need with acts of caring and compassion. . . .The second source is *practice, the doing of caring.* . . . For caring to become a lasting disposition, the practice of it ought to be in the range of once a week throughout childhood and adolescence. . . . Service should be a mainstay of developmental experience, being highly valued and promoted in family, congregation, school, clubs, teams and organizations."[5]

So kids need to see you serve, and they need to participate in service. But can you force an uninterested child to serve? Think about the way you get them to eat vegetables—you make them appetizing and you spruce up their favorite kind of vegetable. As parents and grandparents, we make service doable by having them serve alongside us and by finding appropriate, interesting avenues of service for them.

Simple Ways to Build Empathy

The chapters in the second section, Ideas to Get You Started, will provide concrete suggestions for connecting with others, building empathy, and developing a sense of God's worldwide purposes. Parents can further build a foundation of empathy through general life experiences such as the following.

Modeling empathy in anger. When parents stop in their anger to consider how a child feels, children become recipients of grace and learn from this. They see what it means to set aside anger and opinions and think about how the other person feels.

Love of pets and plants. Small children especially can begin to learn empathy through caring for their pets and for the flowers that grow in their yard. Instead of crushing a spider, we can help children put it outside. Empathy means moving gently through life so as not to dominate other living things. Living things should not be crushed or mistreated.

Caring for extended family. If grandparents or great-grandparents live close by, checking in on them and meeting their needs teaches empathy. Otherwise, you may wish to "adopt" an older friend as a grandparent. Kent and Mary Price saw their children develop empathy when their family, including their two daughters, decided to welcome Granny to live with them. Mary tells how Granny couldn't drive her car anymore and had been widowed for four years. "We asked her to choose a way to live so she could live closer to us. She decided to sell her home and add on to our home. For a year, she lived in our guest room and we had to adjust to sharing our space." The family had to consider her needs in sharing bathrooms, the television, and the living areas. This was quite an adjustment for all, but Mary says it helped them learn to consider the needs of others.

> *A child growing in empathy is moving from isolation to connection, from self-centeredness to others-awareness, from hostility to hospitality.*

Asking children questions is a positive way to teach empathy. Adults tend to talk about issues of the poor and oppressed and missions in a preachy or guilt-producing way, but empathetic questions work better. When you consider that the average person in a developing nation lives in a dwelling not as posh as most garages, you might ask a child, "What would it be like to live in a garage? How would that be different for a family of five?" This approach works better than quoting statistics to a child.

In violence-prevention programs, kids evaluate solutions to problems by asking, "How would others feel about your solution?" Asking a young child, "How do you think Johnny felt when you said that?" prepares him or her to hear you ask later, "How do you think that homeless person felt when . . . ?"

An opportune time to ask questions is when a new child enters your child's class. (That newcomer is the equivalent of the "stranger" in Matthew 25:35, 43). You can ask, "Do you remember what it was like to be the new kid? Do you remember not having any friends—not knowing someone to eat lunch with? That's probably how this child feels."

When children's items are stolen or friends reject them, ask, "How do you feel about that? What would you like to see happen?" (Keeping a "feelings" chart with faces on the refrigerator helps. When you can't get the kids in your life to say how they feel, say, "Just point to the feeling you have.") Eventually, you'll be able to transfer this awareness of feelings to others' situations. For example, when you see television news about refugees driven from their homeland, say, "Remember how you felt when. . . . That's how these people probably feel."

Connecting a circumstance with a personal acquaintance. When you and your children hear unjustly derisive comments about a person or group, bring up someone they know with a similar experience. If someone says all poor people are lazy, you can say that some poor people are probably lazy, but Mr. and Mrs. X at church (someone they know who seems "normal") went through hard times. The church brought them groceries and paid their rent for a while, and now they are on their feet again. Suppose you hear a news report reproaching Haiti's tremendous debt. Remind the children about Ms. Y who was a missionary there for many years and witnessed people so hungry they ate bark off the trees.

Venturing beyond their world. Jeff Wright, executive director of the

Center for Anabaptist Leadership, explains that kids develop empathy when they encounter kids from different backgrounds in safe situations where they can fully hear one another. "At a camp where kids of several ethnic backgrounds attended, the Asian kids told about being graded harder in school; the others didn't believe them. Then black kids told about being followed in stores because they were suspected of shoplifting; the others didn't believe them. They finally began believing each other and seeing life through the other kids' eyes."

From Hostility to Hospitality

A child growing in empathy is moving from isolation to connection, from self-centeredness to others-awareness, from hostility to hospitality. Hospitality is a huge concept, and having people for dinner is only a small part. Being hospitable to a stranger involves reaching out to someone who is unfamiliar, speaks another language, has another skin color, wears different sorts of clothes, lives a lifestyle unlike ours, or makes us afraid.

Hospitable people create spaces in their life for strangers, making it easy for them to reveal themselves.

When Abraham received three strangers at Mamre and offered them water, bread and a fine tender calf, they *revealed themselves* to him as the Lord announcing that Sarah his wife would give birth to a son (Gen. 18:1-15). When the widow of Zarephath offered food and shelter to Elijah, he *revealed himself* as a man of God offering her an abundance of oil and meal and raising her son from the dead (1 Kings 17:9-24). When the two travelers to Emmaus invited the stranger who had joined them on the road to stay with them for the night, Jesus *made himself known* in the breaking of the bread as their Lord and Saviour (Luke 24:13-35). When hostility is converted into hospitality then fearful strangers can become guests revealing to their hosts the promise they are carrying with them.[6] [my italics]

Going out of our way to welcome people is not convenient. When the Prices told me they traveled from Nashville to Mexico City for the wedding of Mary's brother, the Scrooge in me thought, What an expensive trip for an entire family! Since the couple was coming back to the United States to live, why bother going all that way? I said nothing, but Mary explained: "We didn't know her, but we knew she was leaving her family to come to the United States. We knew she'd feel isolated here since she didn't speak English. I thought she was brave, so we wanted to welcome her and get to know her."

Mary and her daughter Laura went on to describe the beautiful wedding and the different customs of the culture. They enjoyed the celebration even though they couldn't speak Spanish or talk to anyone. As I listened, I thought, This is how people spend money when welcoming strangers is important to them.

Empathy begins with eye contact. Several years ago Jack and Elizabeth Shepherd walked across America on a "missionary journey" as homeless persons befriending the homeless. Jack told me what it was like to wake up in a cardboard box every morning and have no one look you in the eyes for days: "When you walk down the street and people look at you with hatred, fear, and a condescending attitude, the tips of your shoes become a nice sight. The biggest thing you can give a homeless person isn't a place to stay or a job or a bathroom. It's a smile. You can recognize them as a human being."

A smile is an appropriate symbol of empathy: smiling at the person who struggles with her accent to make herself understood; smiling at the pride of our sponsored child in Sri Lanka as she writes us in the circular letters of her Sinhalese language; smiling as I tell my kids the latest good news of rehabilitation from the Samaritan Center. For a minute, I live in another person's world, and it isn't so strange after all.

QUESTIONS FOR CONSIDERATION

Choose a few of the following questions to discuss with others or to ponder yourself.

1. Underline the qualities or experiences of Holocaust rescuers that you experienced while growing up.

Qualities or Characteristics	*Experiences*
Adventuresome	Being marginalized, left out, or
Ability to speak up	undervalued
Ability to examine prejudices	Exposed to suffering at an early
Empathetic imagination (imag-	age
ining the effect of a negative	Cooperating to promote the
situation on a person)	well-being of others
	Having a morally strong parent
	with whom you felt close
	Living in a home where hospi-
	tality was highly valued
	Belonging to a group that
	valued compassion

Did these experiences make you more compassionate?
Circle any you wish you had experienced.

2. Which qualities would you most like to cultivate in your children? Which experiences would you most like to give your children?

3. Which of the following ways of teaching children empathy seem most doable to *you*? Put a check mark by them:

    ❑ asking children questions, such as, What would you do?
    ❑ taking your child to visit someone who is looked down on by friends or family
    ❑ talking with someone who is hurting or helping the person in some practical way
    ❑ caring for pets and plants
    ❑ caring for extended family
    ❑ connecting a world event or situation with a personal acquaintance

❑ venturing out beyond their world on outings with family, school, or youth group
❑ smiling and greeting a homeless person

PERSONAL DEVOTIONS

Reread the story of Jesus' interaction with Legion (Luke 8:26-39). Look at the above list of qualities, characteristics, and experiences of Holocaust rescuers. Which of these qualities do you see in Jesus?

PRAYER. Show me, O God, what it means to be adventuresome and bold to speak up for you. Also teach me empathy and the ability to feel with others who are nothing like me. Amen.

FAMILY DEVOTIONS

In everything do to others as you would have them do to you.
—Matthew 7:12

PRAYER. O God, give us the wisdom to be able to imagine how we would like others to treat us. Give us insight into how others want to be treated. We may not be able to do that, but show us how to do it a little better. Amen.

From Self-Protective to Proactive

E ven if we're convinced we want our children to reach out and help, something inside us says, Play it safe, or, Nobody expects children to give of themselves. I caught myself thinking those things when Earl Martin told me what had happened when he and his wife, Pat, had volunteered to invite a city girl their daughter's age to stay for a week. Their guest, Crystal, and their daughter, Lara, bonded quickly.

The week was delightful for everyone. At the week's end, however, Earl and Pat were a bit stunned when six-year-old Lara announced she wanted to give Crystal her favorite doll.  This doll was special, because Lara's grandmother had given the same kind of doll to each granddaughter. All I could think was, What would you tell Grandma? Earl said, "We asked Lara to think about it overnight. We suggested she give Crystal her brand new book of Mother Goose stories, or we could buy Crystal something special. The next morning, Lara was still eager to give her treasured doll to Crystal. With some poignancy, we permitted her to do so. We felt we could not inhibit this generous instinct within Lara." (They told Grandma several years later.)

When I told Pat what I'd been thinking, she understood my feeling: "This was a powerful reminder that we as parents can inhibit the natural compassion children sometimes have." Kids sense our feelings that compassionate actions are unnecessary, and they learn "to restrain their charitable instincts and be realistic."[1]

Our role as parents and grandparents, then, is to help children find ways to practice compassion that are wise, safe, and realistic. With our forethought, kids can be exposed to the heartbreak of poverty and the need for the gospel message without being terrified. The key is to focus on positive things that are happening and get involved. This is one more way to show them how God *so loves* me and how God also *so loves* the world.

This proactive stance keeps kids from a self-centered view of faith. "Too often a child's world view goes something like this: 'God loves me. God blesses me. Jesus will help me in time of trouble.' In contrast, a Biblical world view says, 'God blesses me so that I may be a blessing to all of His creation.' Abraham, in Genesis (12:1-3), was *blessed to be a blessing*. . . . A Biblical world view reveals this common thread tying together the Bible from Genesis to Revelation: God's mission is to reach all people with the Good News of Jesus Christ. God brings us into partnership . . . and then blesses us, not just for our own benefit, but so that we can bless others, both spiritually and physically."[2]

This world view is a radical shift from counting on God to solve my problems and expecting church services to make me feel good. Faith is rooted in a relationship with God, and I get to partner with the Creator of the universe in redeeming the world.

Sound too lofty? Redemption always involves pulling people back from their slide into sin and despair, as Christ's death on the cross, the ultimate redeeming act, did. We can show our children how they can participate in redeeming others—even in small ways. Conversing with nursing home residents may pull them back from despair. Responding to news about a flood or famine by praying for the victims and sending a check (a child can do a chore to contribute) is redemptive.

Kent and Mary Price pulled their children into redemptive activity when they let them participate in their church's night to house the homeless. Mary felt this was "a safe place for the business of caring. The people have been screened for violence or mental unsuitability.

We go there to spend time with people in need, participate in meal preparation, and pack a sack lunch for next day."

One particular night, as then ten-year-old Laura Price sat down to eat vegetable soup and watch "Seinfeld" with some of the guests, she got to talking to one of the men. Later he asked Laura if she would write to his daughter, who was her age. "It was Christmas time and he missed them [his family]," Laura explained. "He hadn't seen her in a long time. He wanted her to know he was OK. He was afraid that if he wrote, they'd burn his letter." Laura wrote to her, but the letter came back. Still, Laura said she was glad she had tried. Even though it wasn't a "success," Laura got to interact with the man and show she cared. That was the point of her being there.

Is it OK to bring children along and let them see hurt and disappointment this way? The Prices prepared their children for what they might see or hear, so they wouldn't be uncomfortable. Mary explained, "We didn't want them to be judgmental. Our purpose was to stay open as to how we might be caring, not to ask a lot of questions about why they were there." It works better than you might think, because sometimes a ten-year-old can talk less self-consciously to strangers than an adult can.

Going the Extra Mile

For Jesus, love was about being intentional and proactive. It wasn't enough not to hate the enemy. When his friend sliced off the ear of the high priest's slave, Jesus healed the ear of his enemy's slave. Jesus teaches us to fight fire not with fire but with a shocking amount of water.

For us, it's not enough to refrain from making fun of the guy begging in front of the grocery store; we need to buy him a loaf of bread. It's not enough to be proud of our church's sending missionaries; we need to get to know them and pray for them. It's not enough to be racially tolerant; we need to be reconcilers, promoting racial reconciliation.

Going the extra mile means rubbing shoulders with and serving those who are different from ourselves. Earl Martin talks about bridging that gap: "Sometimes we fear what it would mean for us to get too involved with people who are strangers to us. The first Christmas Eve that we lived in our present house, a barn next door to us caught fire. A family was living in a house trailer inside the barn, and they lost everything. They had made their living by following the circus. Some people called them gypsies, I believe.

"So for Christmas Day we suddenly had another family living in our house. We put a sign out front saying that if neighbors wanted to share in the family's loss, they could leave gifts on the front porch. By the end of Christmas Day, the porch was filled with clothing, toys, and food. The family stayed with us a week or so until they found a place to live."

The Martins now remember that year as one of their favorite Christmases. "We loved their presence with us. This unexpected event reminded us all that our lives are enriched when we take time to sit down with folks who are very different from us and hear their heartbeat."

Compassion without Nightmares

How do we acquaint children with the world's great needs without upsetting them? How do we expose them to suffering at an early age (one of the ten rescuers' characteristics), yet with appropriate boundaries? Here are some clues.

Offer hope. Information about troublesome situations has to be tempered with a sense that someone is doing something about them, Virginia Hostetler, a mother of two, pointed out. "Yes, the world's in awful shape, and there are problems, but caring people are trying to solve them." Her husband, Michael, adds, "We don't try to create a false world, but we focus on something we can build on."

Uncover interesting stories. The story of Trevor Ferrell amazes kids. At the age of eleven, Trevor "saw a TV news clip about the homeless in Philadelphia. He talked his father into driving him through areas where the homeless hang out. At one stop along the way, Trevor jumped out of the car and gave a pillow and blanket to a man sleeping on the streets. From that night, December 8, 1983, to this day, Trevor has not missed a night on the streets.

"The following nights he took food and eventually 'Trevor's Campaign' grew to feed hundreds of people nightly out of a traveling van, open a temporary shelter for up to 40 homeless men, women and children, a thrift shop to collect donations and clothes, and now 'Next Door,'"[3] a comprehensive shelter. Trevor's parents wrote a book about this called *Trevor's Place*, which includes how kids at school taunted him for doing this. (*See* Resources.)

You might protest, That raises my kids' sights too high! Maybe, but "one must think like a hero to behave like a merely decent human being."[4] Stories like Trevor's help kids "think like a hero" and be willing to volunteer alongside you sometime.

Use positive language. Negative clichés, even funny ones, do damage. One of my friend's grandmas used to look at us when we were disheveled from playing and say, "You look like the wild men from Borneo!" After that, Borneo seemed to me to be a place where really dumb people lived. Generalizations such as "savage hordes of Indians" and "dangerous neighborhoods" send negative messages that are difficult for children to erase later. In truth, so-called "dangerous neighborhoods" are full of thousands of sensible parents who are fearful and who want to keep their kids safe, too.

Mix work and play. Insert elements of fun into activities that are charitable or mission-oriented. Let kids bring a friend or go to the beach afterward. When Jim and Susan Vogt wanted to protest a cross that the Ku Klux Klan put up every year in Fountain Square in Cincinnati, they knew it would be difficult for their children to stand in the cold for long periods of time. They solved the dilemma by taking turns holding their sign, "We stand here with the value of loving all people." Off-duty family members took their breaks at the ice-skating rink next door.

How We Get It Wrong

There are so many ways to do good things badly. Here are a few to watch out for.

"Philosophizing" instead of *"philanthropizing."*[5] When the disciples first met the man born blind, they made him the subject of their debate, while Jesus saw him as a candidate for compassion (John 9:1-41). After Jesus miraculously healed the man, the Pharisees didn't rejoice that he could see; rather, they tormented both his parents and him with questions, and finally kicked him out of the synagogue.

Quibbling often replaces real help. For example, people debate about the "deserving poor" versus the "nondeserving poor," while the Gospels offer no distinction. Jesus didn't skip healing undeserving persons while helping the deserving ones. The scriptural injunction is against idleness: "Anyone unwilling to work should not eat" (2 Thess. 3:10). Not all poor people are lazy, and not all employed people are industrious. Scripture simply indicts those who don't give (even with excellent excuses) and applauds those who bestow their God-given blessings onto others with an open heart.

Self-congratulation. When my kids and I first befriended Ethel, I felt like Lady Bountiful. Clerks would start to shoo her out of the thrift store, and I would smugly say, "She's OK. She's with me."

Reading and meditating on the Gospels (and relating them to our children) helps us get over ourselves. After Jesus healed a certain man, he said, Don't tell anybody!, not Let's hold a press conference (Matt. 8:4). Jesus was glad to promote others, not himself.

How We Get It Right

Be honest about shortcomings. As I worked on curriculum about world poverty for a nonprofit organization, I tripped over tragic statistics that rang bells in my life. For example, Ecuador's infant mortality rate (the number of infants under the age of one who die per thousand) is over five times higher than the rate in the United States, where I live.[6] Why? In developing countries women have limited access to prenatal care and immunizations for their babies. Uhm . . . as a young mother, I complained about taking horse pill–sized pregnancy vitamins and waiting in line with a baby and toddler to get free immunizations at the clinic. While working on the curriculum, I saw that those inconvenient tablets and hectic mornings secured a hardiness for my children that kids in developing countries sorely need.

I read a story about a mother who didn't have ten dollars for a visit to the doctor or transportation to get there. I had complained about waiting in a doctor's office. I also had complained about utility bills, while other families cooked with cow dung and died of the parasites transmitted to their food. I had complained about paying water bills, yet less-than-clean water passes on diseases, making it a primary culprit in those thirty-five thousand deaths of children every day from preventable disease. I had complained about going to the grocery store, yet there I bought nutritious, affordable food, much more than rice and beans, that kept my children from being malnourished as half the world is.

These realizations caused a turnaround in me. I had complained about the things that saved my kids' lives! I had been so unaware of my advantages that I had discounted them. I saw now how wide the gap was between my world and the world of others. This new vision gave me a strong desire to help.

Stay tied to the heart of Christ. In quiet moments of prayer, God showed me my invisible barriers: Certain disabilities put me off; having to ask someone with an accent to repeat herself annoyed me; I prided myself in helping a missionary family. I noticed these things only when I heard God speak to me about them in prayer.

A discipline such as prayer keeps us tied to the heart of Christ. Christine Sine served as a doctor on a mercy ship for twelve years. She is now forced to live in the United States because of a chronic disease. When I interviewed her, I asked, "How do you stay passionate—now that you're a normal person like me?" She answered by describing a mix of spiritual disciplines—Bible reading, spiritual reading, service, prayer:

It is difficult to keep my priorities right when I live in the

United States. I have found several keys that remind me what is really important from God's perspective.

1. I read the Gospels regularly and continually ask myself the question, How did Christ live and how would he live in our present age? I need to work with great intentionality for transformation in my life so that it is geared towards making "God's purposes my purposes"—sight for the blind, release for the prisoners, and good news to the poor.

2. On a regular basis, I read books that challenge me to "live more simply so that others may simply live." [*See* Resources.]

3. My husband and I stay connected with groups that work in overseas missions and try to spend as much time as possible with people who are immersed in these needs.

4. We try to take one trip to a Third World country each year. There is no better way to keep our eyes on what is really important than to constantly expose ourselves to the challenges of the world around us.

5. We want to get involved in a local urban project amongst the poor. This would connect us to the needs of our own communities and give us an opportunity to work alongside others who do.

6. We take one to two days every few months for a prayer retreat. This is not a time to pray for others but to focus on our relationship to God. We examine whether the things we think should be priorities in our lives occupy most of our time and energy.

Having looked at the distractions from compassionate behavior we face, the biblical mandate for compassion, and the importance of empathy and proactive zeal, we're ready to move into the practical chapters. As you read the following chapters, you may think, Will my kids "get it"? Let me pass on some reassurance given to me. It's true your role as a parent is limited. You only plant the seed, but Gretchen Lovingood, whose children are now grown, assures us that eventually, they do get it: "We live in Santa Barbara and my children had a lot of affluent friends, but they didn't do the things their friends did. We told them, 'We're calling you to be different, but in the end, it's up to you.' Eventually, it clicks."

One of those "click" moments occurred for Steve Lovingood after he was away from home and in the Coast Guard. He'd been taught that people were the same all over the world, but . . . were they? "He was working in the Bering Sea, watching Russian fishing boats," relates Gretchen. "As he focused on one ship through his binoculars, he looked into a Russian sailor's eyes. They looked at each other through their binoculars for just one split second. Steve told us, 'I was one person in America, he was one person in Russia. A light bulb came on. He's a human being like me.'"

Enjoy.

QUESTIONS FOR CONSIDERATION

Choose a few of the following questions to discuss with others or to ponder yourself.

1. Underline what you believe is the one best key word in each of the world views below. Compare your ideas with other members of the group.

   Typical world view: God loves me. God blesses me. Jesus will help me in time of trouble.

   Biblical world view: God brings us into partnership and then blesses us, not just for our own benefit but so that we can bless others, both spiritually and physically.

2. Can you think of a time when you've been involved in a "redemptive" activity—pulling someone back from a slide into sin and despair?

3. Going the extra mile means rubbing shoulders with and serving those who are different from you. Give an example of what going the extra mile would look like in your life.

4. The principle of mixing work with play is an important one in growing compassionate kids. Think of an example of service and how you could mix fun with, before, or after it.

5. If you were to choose to do one of the six disciplines described by Christine Sine at the end of the chapter (p. 52), which one would you pick?

PERSONAL DEVOTIONS

For those who want to save their life will lose it, and those who lose their life for my sake, and for the sake of the gospel, will save it. For what will it profit them to gain the whole world and forfeit their life?

—Mark 8:35-36

PRAYER. O God, Jesus' example of radical love is too difficult for me. I'm afraid I'll lose too much if I love that much. Give me courage to experiment with losing my life in you. Amen.

FAMILY DEVOTIONS

I will make of you a great nation, and I will bless you, and make your name great, so that you will be a blessing. . . . In you all the families of the earth shall be blessed.

—Genesis 12:2-3

Ask the children in your life,
- How has our family been blessed? (Inquire about physical, material, emotional blessings.)
- How can our family be a blessing to others in the neighborhood? to others on this earth?

Don't be concerned about having answers. It's good to ask questions first and let them sit in the air.

PRAYER. Thank you, great God, for your blessings of _____. Show us how to use these blessings to bless others on this earth. Amen.

Ideas to Get You Started

chapter six

Conversations within the Natural Course of Family Life

You may be wondering, Isn't there a class where my kids could learn compassion for the world? Then you wouldn't have to do this. It would be done. Period. Such a class would be helpful, but actually there is a better method: Parents and grandparents feed children bits of healing information and homestyle empathy in incremental doses day after day.

One of the best settings for bite-sized information and inspiration is casual conversations within the family. In those conversations, kids can ask questions that widen their circle of what and who are cool.

Off-the-cuff conversations create an environment in which those characteristics of empathetic Holocaust rescuers can grow. First, children get to listen to you and identify with you as a "morally strong" parent. Sure, they *seem* to ignore what you say, but they'll repeat your exact words to their friends. In family discussions, kids get to "examine their own prejudices" in the safety of a loving environment. If you don't dominate the conversation and you allow them plenty of time to talk, they'll "present themselves, speak up, and be persuasive" (another rescuer skill).

Driving together in the car offers opportunities to observe how life is lived on other socioeconomic levels. While carpooling, one of my daughter's friends said she'd heard that a kid at school lived in a garage. The other kids snickered and joked about cooking dinner on the lawn mower. I said, "Living in a garage is pretty common." The kids looked surprised, so I continued: "More than half of the people in the world live in a space as small as a garage, only it's built much worse. Living in homes like ours is rare on this planet." Knowing I was laying heavy-duty information on them, I quipped, "So by the world's standards, we're a bunch of rich people." They liked that last idea.

Virginia Hostetler uses the vast time spent in the car to let her children listen to taped Bible stories. When one tape mentioned the "enemies of the Israelites" several times, Virginia asked her kids, "Did God love the enemies of the Israelites?" Her son, Stefan, said, "No, God didn't." So she talked with her kids about how God loves so-called "good people" and "bad people."

A question Virginia frequently asks her kids is this one: "Who does God love?" because, she says, "Many U.S. citizens have repeated the phrase 'one nation under God' so often that they think we're the one nation God loves. They think God is on our side all the time. Kids miss that God loves all people and that we can share God's love with all people."

Susan Vogt says her family tried formal discussions on topics of compassion, but that approach didn't work. "So we try to weave information more naturally into conversations," says Susan. "Jim or I will bring up what we read in the newspaper or something we heard about at work. We say, 'I heard about. . . . What do you think? What would you have done if you were in this situation?'"

One evening Susan mentioned the man she sees on her way home from work. He holds a sign that reads: "Will work for food." She asked the kids, "What should I have done?" They talked about how some people might have gone to McDonald's and bought food. One kid asked, "What if he doesn't have legitimate need?" Another responded, "Are we the ones to judge?"

Susan says, "So we asked, 'Is it sometimes OK to make a mistake and give a job or food to someone who was manipulating you?' As a whole, we decided it's better to be used sometimes than to pass up an opportunity to help."

Props Help

A certain prop that helped the Vogts was a map of the world on their dining room wall. When Heidi Vogt was sixteen, she wrote about it.

LATITUDE

by Heidi Vogt

A very large map covers my dining room wall—ceiling to floor, corner to corner. It is laminated, so as never to get damaged by the elements. White clocks lining the top show time changes, and the continents are varying shades of green and yellow except for Greenland, which is (ironically) white. Parts have been scratched out and written over ("Union of Soviet Socialist Republics" now has "Commonwealth of Independent States" above it in black marker). And the space between latitude lines gets bigger from bottom to top—creating the illusion that Greenland is bigger than South America, which I've now been told isn't true. I can't think of a time when one-fourth of my dining room *hasn't* been a two-dimensional geography lesson. It's amazing how much a wall can shape one's life.

When I was in sixth grade, I had to memorize all the capital cities of Europe. I told my parents about the assignment over dinner. "Why Europe?" asked my father from across the table, "Why not the other continents too?"

I had no answer. I had never considered why we learned about some countries and not others. But my father was determined to help me think about it.

"Tell me one country in Africa and its capital," he said. "I don't think you'll be able to." Unwilling to admit my ignorance, I looked at the map. First, I pretended to be thinking and strained my eyes at the small print a few feet away from me—trying to make out a word that could be an African capital. But it was an old trick my parents knew well, so my dad immediately added, "*Without* looking at the map." I looked around the table for assistance, but no one came to my aid by mouthing a clue. Finally, I was obliged to admit my defeat and return quietly to my dinner.

"I'll give you five dollars if you memorize all the countries in Africa and their capitals," my father challenged. Five dollars can be a fortune—to a sixth grader! I thought of all the gum and candy I could buy. My father definitely knew how to motivate me! That night I copied all the countries and capitals down onto a piece of yellow filler paper, determined to win what had now become a bet.

I lost. I never got all the capitals of Africa memorized—although I *did* learn about half and I *did* memorize all the capitals of Europe. The five dollars lost its charm after I realized how much work I would have to put in.

Also, in the middle of it all, I decided I had already learned what I needed to. Sitting there, reciting "Zaire, Kinshasa; Liberia, Monrovia; Senegal, Dakar," I realized that my father had taught me a lesson bigger than a list of countries on a paper—I wasn't going to learn everything I needed, or wanted, to learn at school. Those teachers might leave big gaps in my knowledge if I left it all up to them. I realized my education was up to me.

I also discovered a whole world out there—not just a few countries in Europe. I saw that just because my ancestry is European doesn't mean other countries don't have history just as important to the making of our world. It led me to explore, to discover other countries and cultures on my own. The map on my dining room wall is a constant reminder of this fact for me.

Now when I look at that tattered specimen, it brings back all kinds of memories. I recall "family nights" spent looking at the map and discussing "places of conflict in the world" (as my father described them) and what we could do to help. I remember the places on that map that I've had the opportunity to visit—the trips to Italy, France, and Russia that our family couldn't really afford but decided the experience was more important than money. The map has become something much bigger, something that would never fit on a dining room wall. It has become a quadrilateral testament to the world view that my parents have passed on to me—a view that peace, justice, and understanding in our world should be important to us. After all, what's the use of a big map without big ideas to accompany it?[1]

Other families have used wall maps as well, putting dots on the locations of missionaries the children have met. Such a map, ever-present in a child's world, imparts to that child an ongoing awareness, and it provides you a prop to refer to whenever you need it.

Conversing with a Child

Adults tend to sermonize to children rather than converse with them. It's important not to talk *at* kids but to talk *with* them. Susan Vogt keeps the talking casual by looking for situations in columns by Ann Landers or Dear Abby and asking: "What advice would you give this person?" Heidi, now twenty-two, says the children would groan whenever their mother asked that question (they caught on!), but she remembers, "It affects you after a while, and you think about things differently."

After you ask a question, you have to hold back. Don't jump in and tell the kids what you think. "If they answered, 'I don't know,' Jim or I would offer an outlandish answer to get them thinking," says Susan Vogt. For example, we've brought up that when Heidi leaves home, we may go down to one car since Jim works at home. That would mean our son Aaron, who doesn't drive, would have to take the bus or car-pool. We've even discussed sharing a second car with another family. This topic really gets the kids going, because they don't like riding the bus. We may not ever go down to one car, but our discussions of how it helps the environment and so on are good. We hope it's impacted their thinking."

Conversations are valuable because they're so casual within everyday life. If, while watching football or washing dishes, you mention a missionary or a "place of conflict in the world," it breaks down the walls between normal moments and moments when you have an opportunity to be compassionate.

When compassion is woven into mundane moments of life, kids don't become adults who find being compassionate odd outside the walls of the church. Our children are less likely to become like the goat-people in Matthew 25 who said (roughly), "Lord, if we had known it was you, at least we would have formed a Social Action Committee!"[2] Instead, since our kids live with an awareness of the joys and sorrows of others now, they will be able, as adults, to bring compassion into conversation and to be a "morally strong parent" for their children.

QUESTIONS FOR CONSIDERATION

Choose a few of the following questions to discuss with others or to ponder yourself.

1. Which settings for conversations would work best with the children in your life?
   ❑ in the car
   ❑ at the dinner table
   ❑ while watching the news

2. What props might be helpful: a world map, pictures on the refrigerator, jewelry from another country?

PERSONAL DEVOTIONS

Hebrew parents displayed the words of God "as a sign on your hand," "an emblem on your forehead," and "on the doorposts of your house and on your gates" (Deut. 11:18, 20). God's words permeated all of life.

Conversations within the Natural Course of Family Life

Close your eyes and imagine the places in your home where you could have brief conversations about issues of compassion with the children in your life.

PRAYER. O God of the ordinary and mundane, show me how to live and breathe your compassion in the conversations in my home. Amen.

Making the News Meaningful

M any families have shut off the television news or quit reading the newspaper because the news is too "terrible." As we teach our children what it means to love God who *so loves* the world, we need to care about what happens to this world. Rather than ignoring the news, then, it is better to pay attention to it with the agenda of Christ: bringing good news to the poor, letting the oppressed go free.

You can fuel those car and dinner table conversations by reading the newspaper with a heart for world events. At times, I've cut out articles and photos from the newspaper, underlining the most poignant sentence or paragraph. (That helps me be brief!) You may want to set a child on your lap so she can hear and read too.

One key to using news stories effectively is to look for kid-friendly details. Smells and odors attract kids' interest. I once read about how the trash dumps in Tijuana smelled, and we talked about what it would be like to live there. (Of course, one of my kids was sure the dump smelled better than the other's room.) Statistics about what a fast-food hamburger costs in other countries usually surprise kids. Explain that because a consumer in developing countries typically has much less income, buying a hamburger is like our buying a new basketball or a pair of shoes.

Since a frequent parent-kid topic is chores, I saved a picture from *World Vision* magazine of a child hauling water. During dinner, we talked about what hauling water would be like, and I tried to work their imagination. What if the bucket broke? What if you were barefoot and stepped on something with all the weight of the water in your hands? What if you slipped and spilled it? What if your big brother tripped you and you spilled it? asked my daughter. I carefully avoided comments such as, "You think you've got it bad!" My goal was to build empathy for kids around the world, not to make my children feel guilty.

As kids mature, don't be afraid to share horrors as appropriate. I got upset reading about the land mines left in Afghanistan after the war. Because these small land mines looked like butterflies, children picked them up and were maimed or killed when they exploded. When I told this to my family, I showed them a picture from the article—a one-legged child with a crutch. We agreed to send our small, monthly "poor and oppressed/missions" donation to an organization that was defusing these mines.

Be sure to share items of hope too. Recently I read about Tom Leyden, a former skinhead leader who "first came to the Simon Weisenthal Center years ago, . . . not to learn about the Holocaust [about which this center teaches], but to admire his heroes." That was a few years ago. "Today he works for the National Task Force Against Hate for the Simon Weisenthal Center."[1] I saved this information and read a paragraph of it to my family at dinner. I wanted them to see how people can turn around.

Talking about the news this way works only if you aren't preachy. The best insurance against preachiness is to let the news touch you. Let newspaper reading and radio news listening become a time to pray for peace and justice and the spread of the gospel. Your kids will see that your concern about current events comes from your heart.

Unusual Sources of News

Mission magazines. Before throwing away mission magazines, newsletters, and fundraising appeals, look for a good story. Sure, the war in Rwanda was about struggles for political power, but it also involved a girl named Maroshema who saw her father murdered by militia men. She decided to become a soldier herself and kill. Then, Compassion International began taking care of her—providing food and clothing, teaching her about Christ and giving her trauma counseling. Maroshema began healing and learning about God, learning to pray, and thinking about a more hopeful future.[2] Such examples of redemption show kids the heart of Christ.

Since my kids are interested in sports, I brought to the dinner table an article from *Global Prayer Digest* about a 1996 Olympics participant, Addis Gezahegn. She's a beautiful young woman from Ethiopia, and in 1992 she was the first female athlete ever to represent Ethiopia in the Olympics.

Nine years earlier, Addis had been a child sponsored through a mission organization (our family has sponsored several children, so this fact interested my kids). The faithful check from Addis Gezahegn's sponsor provided school fees, clothing, and medical care, as well as seed grain for planting and agricultural training, so that her family could grow an adequate food supply. The sponsorship program also guided her to a strong faith in Christ, which she said was "the best gift."[3] At the dinner table grace that evening, we prayed for Addis Gezahegn.

This story provided the opening to tell my kids that among the nations participating in the 1996 Olympics there

Let newspaper reading and radio news listening become a time to pray for peace and justice and the spread of the gospel.

were forty-seven Islamic nations that are closed to the gospel. Even Iraq sent a soccer team to Atlanta. Christian organizations witnessed to these visiting nations through coffee houses, sports clinics, and children's programs. My kids were surprised—missionaries do cool stuff!

Missionaries. When missionaries come to your church, ask them about the news events in their area. They have insights about the news you don't hear elsewhere. Long after the civil war in Rwanda, a missionary visited our church and told us about the desperate poverty and continuing conflicts there. He was gathering tools to ship to Rwanda. Our family, along with our church, was able to help, having learned of the need.

One missionary family keeps in contact with us by E-mail. They often forward us news items. As the war raged on in Kosovo, they forwarded a message about what it was like living through the bombings. Our family was motivated to pray even more for peace.

Watching the News with Kids

Hearing the news isn't just a time of gathering information but also a time for expressing empathy. For example, if Rachel Miller and her kids see news about a flood, she doesn't say, "Gee, look at all that water!" but "Just think how you'd feel if it were our house." Seize such opportunities to develop children's "empathetic imagination" (a quality of rescuers) instead of gawking. When complicated words come up, ask what they mean: What does it mean for people to be *exploited*? to be *oppressed*? to experience *injustice*? What is a *hate crime*?

When we sponsored a child in Bangkok, Thailand, I'd call my kids in to watch any news of Thailand—horrific weather or political fighting. Since the kids were teens by this time, I even shared news stories about young girls from the hills who are led into prostitution to feed the sex tour industry, of which Bangkok is the capital. These stories taught us all about the environment in which our sponsored child was growing up, and we prayed for his purity.

Is exposure to this kind of grim news too much? Holocaust rescuers were "exposed to suffering at an early age." If information is shared with your compassionate perspective, it builds kids' capacity for compassion.

Another way to make information from faraway, obscure cultures kid-friendly is to compare it with something from their experience. Our own experience of an earthquake became a doorway to thinking about people a world away.

Although we lived only nine miles from the epicenter of the 1994 Northridge earthquake, our home was back to normal within a few weeks. Within six months, our freeway had been rebuilt. Within a year, most of the destroyed homes in our neighborhood had been rebuilt. A few lots, however, remained in rubble, because the owners were unable to take advantage of FEMA (Federal Emergency Management Agency) resources.

As we drove past these eyesores every day, I griped. Then I read about how developing countries take years to recover from disasters, because they don't have the money and construction materials we have. I saw that I am one of the "rich in this . . . world" with a responsibility to "be generous and willing to share" (1 Tim. 6:17,18, NIV).

The tattered homes then became huge visual aids to show the disparity of wealth among nations. Every time I wanted to gripe, I reminded myself, within the hearing of anyone in the car, that if this were a developing nation, these houses would not be repaired for years. I explained that we didn't need to feel guilty, but we needed to see that as members of God's family business, we must reach out to people.

Sometimes the events on the news touch you so deeply that you must do something. Susan Vogt has felt that way many times, especially during the Kosovo conflict. "I didn't want to support killing and fighting, yet I could not be a 'guilty bystander,' doing nothing. I got word that a local group was collecting packets of goods for adults and children in Kosovo—diapers, antibiotic ointment, bandages, small stuffed animals, emergency candles. We talked with our kids about that. We agreed to search the house for these things—going through our candle supply and donating a stuffed animal. Each of us would also donate some money.

With this money, we bought cloth diapers, and our family put together some packets. The teen group at our church did more of them. We took them to a central place and had a prayer service as they were collected."

Getting Past Our Own Information Anxiety

What if the news and world events just seem too complicated? "Information anxiety"—having access to more information than a person can possibly absorb—is not uncommon. A weekday edition of the *New York Times,* for example, contains more information than the average person in seventeenth-century England was likely to come across in a lifetime.[4] No wonder we're overwhelmed!

Consider this. Looking at the news with an eye toward simplifying it for children may be a way to get past "information anxiety." Look for the "one-liner," the one statistic or fact that speaks to you. Read the background, so you're not taking something out of context, then find something that can be easily remembered and repeated.

One-liners can roll off the tongue and be conversational instead of lecture-like. We may even remember them for a long time. From various interviews over the years, here are a few one-liners that have stayed with me:

- *Two-thirds of the world's people eat rice and beans.* This led me to quip, when going through job transitions, that our family was still rich because we ate rice, beans, and had chicken now and then!
- *Twenty percent of the world's population consumes 85 percent of the world's goods.* Remembering that fact led me to draw two pie charts (population, world's goods) on a paper dinner napkin in a restaurant to explain to our kids why we had an eating-out budget.
- *Thirty-five thousand children die every day in developing countries of diseases that are largely preventable.* The idea of "preventable diseases" helped me see the importance of well-baby care, which I had taken for granted.
- *Most people who haven't heard the gospel are in the "10/40*

window." This is an area from 10 degrees latitude north to 40 degrees latitude south. It covers much of northern Africa, the Arab world, India, China, and Indonesia.

These one-liners have a way of flowing into conversations with my kids. I've even overheard my kids repeating these facts to friends.

Using these techniques, we can make the news easier for our children to understand. Even better, we can translate facts into reasons to "let our hearts be broken by the things that break the heart of God."

QUESTIONS FOR CONSIDERATION

Choose a few of the following questions to discuss with others or to ponder yourself.

1. What one-liners or stories, if any, have stuck with you over the years and helped you have compassion for others?

2. What resources, if any, have been most interesting to you: missions magazines, particular missionaries, other?

   Optional: Bring an article from the newspaper or a magazine. Ask the group to help you find the one-liner or come up with kid-friendly details (those related to the five senses) to make the information more accessible.

3. Share with the group any hopeful information you've run across (like the change of heart of former skinhead leader Tom Leyden or the group that gathered goods during the Kosovo conflict).

PERSONAL DEVOTIONS

Rescue the weak and the needy; deliver them from the hand of the wicked.
—Psalm 82:4

PRAYER. Give me eyes, all-seeing God, to notice the stories in the news where the weak and needy are rescued. Let those stories inspire me and give me ideas to help the children in my life. Amen.

Seeing Your Community with Open Eyes

M issions experts agree that a key way to get kids interested in God's work worldwide is to "reach out with your kids where you live—the soup kitchen, the old folks' home. Work together. Let them see your Christianity in action."[1] Then they see that being compassionate is as much a part of life as taking piano lessons, picking up the dry cleaning, and buying new pillows for the sofa.

Reaching out, however, often means going out of your way a bit. Mary Price did this by taking her children to visit nursing homes. Since nursing homes bombard the senses, Mary, who is a nurse, prepared them by saying, "It will look like a hospital and have the funny smells of medicines and cleaning products. It will smell of urine, because many of the people can't control bodily functions. When they need help with the bathroom, the workers can't get there fast enough. If people moan and reach out to touch you, it's because children excite them, and they want to respond. They aren't trying to hurt you. Even though they may not understand what's going on, they still need people to love them."

Mary wanted her children to interact with patients, so she urged them to go in twos, pick out someone, and try to talk to that person. She told them, "First, get on eye level, so they don't have to bend back in the wheelchair. That's being respectful to them. Then introduce yourself and talk to them." She gave them a script of sorts and stood by if they had questions or concerns.

In Life's Normal Moments

Interaction with the voiceless isn't always a matter of going out of your way. Sometimes it's a matter of paying attention to people you might normally ignore or even avoid. For example, Sharon Norris learned not to ignore people who ask for food, especially in the summer when she was off from work and doing things with her boys every day. She and Matthew and Mark developed their own little project. "In the mornings before we left, we packed three or four 'homeless sandwiches.' I used extra grocery money to buy bread and bologna, and if I had more, I got juices too. We also put a tract from our church in each bag." So instead of zooming past people at the freeway exits with signs that said "Will work for food," they stopped and handed them a bag.

A similar idea is keeping "basic bags" in your car to hand out. These plastic bags are filled with a toothbrush, toothpaste, soap, deodorant, shampoo, comb, and a washcloth. Baby powder adds a special touch, because feet that walk that much get awfully tired. If you don't want to hand them out, take them to a shelter.

Sometimes cross-cultural opportunities are right in front of us, and we don't realize it. When Todd Evans gave a Hispanic boy on his sons' soccer team a ride home, he and his boys saw that this child's home was in a tent, alongside other Hispanic families in tents. They were farm workers in the nearby vineyards. His kids were shocked at first, but Todd began recruiting these kids for the soccer team. "Most of the families didn't have the money for soccer uniforms, but the other parents helped out. [Todd admits some parents helped because these kids were such talented soccer players.] Our boys rode to games with them and got to know them. Our family got involved with their kids' families, helping them with applications and insurance forms."

Seeing Your Community with Open Eyes

Understand that certain situations may stretch you in having the heart of Christ. One of Blanca Castro's daughters had a best friend in junior high who gave her head lice. Still, Blanca could not tell her daughter not to socialize with the girl. Blanca says, "I felt bad for her. Her beautiful long hair had to be cut. No one wanted to be around the little girl. I told my daughter, 'Just help her. Go ahead and be her friend.'"

Keep Your Eyes Open

Perhaps someone you know is in need, but you don't realize it. This happened to me with one of my son's teachers, Carol (not her real name). She came to our church, and we became friends. One day when I took my kids over to her apartment, I found her staring into an empty refrigerator and crying over her broken marriage. Before she could pay for rent, food, and child care, her purse was empty. The private school didn't pay much, and she was too devastated by her divorce to manage her money well.

When summer school was over, Carol couldn't find a temporary job that coordinated with child care and bus schedules. I tried to help. I brought her food. I paid her to watch my children. I encouraged her to study for a credential test, so she could get a job in a higher paying school. After several months, Carol disappeared.

A few weeks later, I read in the newspaper that single-parent families were the fastest-growing category among the homeless. A survey of eighty-seven homeless mothers by Harvard Medical School and the University of Southern California[2] pointed out circumstances these women had in common. As I read each one, I saw how Carol and her children fit. In italics below are phrases you might hear in a friendly conversation with a potentially homeless neighbor, friend, or church member. They reflect the common circumstances homeless mothers face.

"My husband is leaving me." "I just moved here." One-third of the surveyed mothers became homeless due to a broken relationship; another third because they were evicted; and another third because they tried to relocate. Carol had just divorced and moved.

"I can pay for everything but child care." Three-fourths of the surveyed mothers couldn't find affordable day care. Until three-year-old Charlie got into school, Carol's day-care bills saddled her.

"I barely knew my parents." "My family can't help." Forty-three percent of the interviewed women were runaways or had been placed in foster or institutional care as children. More than a third of the women had deceased parents, and many had no siblings. Carol's parents were dead; her brother had helped her once but refused to help her again.

"I know I can handle a job, but nothing seems to work out." Sixty percent of the women had at least a high school education, but two-thirds hadn't held a job for longer than a month. It never occurred to me that Carol could be nearly homeless, since she had a master's degree. I didn't understand that her severe loss of self-esteem had made her lethargic at home and on the job. Eventually I discovered from a mutual friend that Carol had been using drugs. That's how bad the despair can get.

You may have other friends who are candidates for homelessness because of these three common situations: they struggle with drug addiction or alcoholism; they suffer from posttraumatic stress disorder (often from serving in Vietnam); they have mental, developmental, or emotional imbalances that require medication. Forty years ago, many in this last group would have been institutionalized.

As affordable housing becomes more difficult to find, it's not so unusual to find someone who is potentially homeless. How can I help? you may wonder. Here are three principles to keep in mind.

1. Be a resource person.

People with financial problems can get so discouraged that they aren't good at digging up job training programs or subsidized child care. Even if you can't offer direct assistance, you can be aware of where to get help.

- Ask among friends about the availability of a reliable used car or inexpensive apartments. Be savvy about employers who offer child care, such as universities and hospitals, which also offer a wide variety of jobs.

- Ask potentially homeless friends to rethink their family options. Can an aunt move in and trade room and board for child care? If they're estranged from family members who might help, probe to see if they could patch things up with their families.
- Know who the people are who know about resources. Large churches often have staff persons who specialize in resources. Some churches publish their own classified ads or bulletin boards that feature used furniture, jobs, and quality day care. A social services resource list may be available at your library. Keep one on hand.

2. Be an encourager.

Treat this person as a friend and peer, not as a needy person. On Carol's birthday, my husband watched her children, while I took her out for cheesecake. It seemed frivolous in light of her serious needs, but she told me how special it made her feel.

Validate the individual. Lack of self-esteem is a major problem. Jan McDougall, chief operations officer of Union Rescue Mission in downtown Los Angeles, told me that almost every woman she works with has been emotionally, sexually, or physically abused by a family member. This is true of many homeless men as well.

We can help bolster self-esteem by pointing out a person's good qualities. When I admired Carol's tall, slim figure in her class picture, she looked shocked. Between the break-up of her marriage and her own self-doubts, she'd forgotten that she was attractive.

Don't expect miracles. Understand that on some days your friend may work on problems but on other days feel hopeless. Carol studied for her credential test sporadically. I tried to praise her for her confident moments and walk with her through the discouraging ones.

77

Find professional support. A family's personal and medical problems may be more than you can handle. Shelters and self-help groups for alcoholics, spouses of alcoholics, and battered women are often listed in the telephone book. Some communities offer free clinics and counseling.

Share your faith. Jan McDougall reminds us that drug pushers are bold and courageous. "We need to be too. I always tell people that God loves them and give them as much input as they can handle."

How do the children in your life figure in all of this? My kids were a part of everything I did with Carol—all a part of the natural course of a day. Just let your kids go along with you.

3. *Don't try to do it all.*

Jan McDougall differentiates between the homeless person who wants help and the "street person" who doesn't. You'll need to help your kids see this distinction as well. "Street people are there by choice, because they like the excitement and the freedom." (Ethel fit this description.) "Most homeless families, however, are people who have lost their jobs and the ability to cope. They have goals, and they'll use whatever help you give them as a stepping-stone to greater things."

Partnering with someone else makes a big difference. Enlist a friend or couple to help, so you're not the sole emotional support for your friends in need. Then the kids in your life can see compassion lived out in other adults' lives as well. I got involved with Carol because my friend Jamie, who was Carol's coworker, asked me to pray for Carol. My kids knew Jamie and respected her, which added to the credibility of what I did.

Turning toward the hungry, needy, and lonely across town or even across the street (instead of away from them) teaches our kids to see the face of Christ in their eyes. These actions also point to those across the globe with similar needs.

QUESTIONS FOR CONSIDERATION

Choose a few of the following questions to discuss with others or to ponder yourself.

1. How are you currently responding to contact with people from a culture that's different from yours—someone from another area, a different socioeconomic level, a different heritage?

2. Which of these activities can you see yourself doing?

    ❑ preparing kids to go to a convalescent home
    ❑ preparing sandwiches or "basic bags" to pass out
    ❑ offering to watch a needy person's children
    ❑ helping someone find an affordable car or apartment

3. If you've tried to help a needy person in the past, how did it go? What did you do that worked that wasn't mentioned in the guidelines above? (Write to Upper Room Books and tell us! You'll find a response card at the back of the book.) Do any of the guidelines above help you see how it might have gone better?

PERSONAL DEVOTIONS

For the Lord does not see as mortals see; they look on the outward appearance, but the Lord looks on the heart.
—1 Samuel 16:7

PRAYER. O God, open my eyes to the needs of the people in front of me. Amen.

FAMILY DEVOTIONS

Religion that is pure and undefiled before God, the Father, is this: to care for orphans and widows in their distress, and to keep oneself unstained by the world.
—James 1:27

Tell your family the story above about Carol (or a story like it). Mention that she was an orphan and resembled a widow, because her children's father was absent from their lives. Explain why it was so startling that she should become homeless.

PRAYER. Help us all, O God, to open our eyes to the needs of those in front of us. Help us to notice details in what is said and done and to reach out in love. Amen.

chapter Nine

World-Class Leisure and Entertainment

While growing compassionate kids will cause you to go "the extra mile" on occasions, it will also challenge you to travel that "first mile" differently from others. A view that God loves all nations will infect your normal life of leisure and entertainment—the way you eat, the gifts you give, and even how you play board games. For example, I know one family who occasionally plays Trivial Pursuit using only the blue section, on geography. These games beef up their familiarity with geography and help them to be more conscious of the world's various cultures.

Another family uses their vacation to attend the Urbana Student Missions Convention. Held every three years, this conference draws more than seventeen thousand students to the campus of the University of Illinois at Urbana-Champaign "for learning, worship, prayer, and discussion about missions and evangelism."[1] These parents take their high school children, not to persuade them to become missionaries but to give them a view of the world based on God's "family business." (*See* Resources.)

Caring about people from other cultures opens us up and helps us accept people who do not look like us or dress like us. Instead of being put off by people who are different, we think they're interesting.

CHAPTER NINE

Eating and Not Eating

Many world-conscious families fix international meals or eat at restaurants that introduce their children to food from different countries. Before eating a Korean meal, Mexican meal, or Indian meal, kids can research such questions as, How do Koreans sit while they eat? Do they use forks, spoons, sticks, fingers? What recipes are used? Is there a special way to set the table?[2]

Holidays present good opportunities to experience other cuisines. Even if you're not Mexican-American, you may want to celebrate Cinco de Mayo (the fifth of May commemorates a Mexican victory over French forces) with tacos and tostados. One Chinese New Year, I helped my daughter's class bake almond cookies.

Ken and Gretchen Lovingood's daughter, Jennifer Guevera, tells about times when their family didn't eat. "We had a hunger meal every Friday of Lent. We ate only bread and water to remind us of people around the world who didn't have food. When I was about twelve, it really got to me. Less than an hour after dinner, I was still hungry! It was easy for me to walk to the refrigerator and get something, but some people had nothing else."

Sometimes a meal like this is called a "famine meal." You serve a meal of plain rice and weak bouillon or tea. If you decide to try a famine meal, prepare the kids in your life by assembling facts and experiences about the starving in the world. Begin the dinner by giving thanks for God's blessings. Even if the kids can come back to the kitchen a few hours later for food, the point is made—people get hungry when they have less to eat!

Leisure Moments

Kids will see their parents as authentically empathetic when even in their "off-duty" moments they are interested in how other people live. As a family, it can be fun to explore other cultures through their drama, art, poetry, and novels. Societies express their pain and aspirations through these art forms. "Christians should listen to the messages these forms convey. Through these mediums, we draw a more accurate picture of our world and thus a more accurate picture of how we may respond."[3]

Such exploration expands a family's world. Everyone better understands "the cultural mosaic of customs, colors, sounds, sights and traditions [as] God's gift to us. Unfortunately, we are often taught to fear what is different to us. This orientation is not biblical. Nor is it [wise]. We become enriched through our encounter with the spectrum of God's handiwork [(other cultures)]—and we become equipped to live effectively and meaningfully in the modern world."[4] That's why adults with wide cross-cultural experiences are now more appealing as candidates for jobs than those with limited experiences.

One example of a way to cross cultures is for those unfamiliar with African-American history to pay attention during February, which is Black History Month. Especially during that time, public television informs and entertains with stories of heroes unknown to many people.

This attention to history is important even for African-American families, because the dominant culture does not showcase black history well. After some scary incidents in public restrooms, Sharon Norris, who is African American, began letting her boys wait for her in the seating area of women's restrooms. One time in a department store, a white woman called the boys "niggers." They didn't understand, because no one had ever called them that name.

Sharon decided to address this knowledge gap by sitting down with her family and watching the video *Rosewood*, a true story about a town in the South during the time of segregation. The blacks in the community were relatively well off but still had to kowtow to whites and look down at the ground when whites spoke to them. A white woman who was beaten by the man with whom she was having an affair accused a black man of beating her. The whites slaughtered almost all the blacks. Sharon says, "My kids asked why that happened, and so I told them how far we had come in this country and what racism was like. I pulled in biblical truth about hatred being wrong."

Choosing videos. Renting videos purposefully can be enriching. At the video store, we came upon the gripping movie *El Norte.* By watching it, we learned how the political systems in other countries can be so oppressive that people risk their lives fleeing them. The movie shows two teenagers fleeing their Latin American country for their lives and struggling as illegal aliens in the United States. I had not understood the realities of life across the border and the desperate lengths to which people—even kids—would go to find freedom.

Movies such as *Out of Africa* and *A Passage to India* expand our world a little, allowing us to see into other cultures. *A Walk in the Clouds* depicts a farm family working hard and loving their land in a way suburbanites can't imagine and perhaps even ridicule. Don't assume kids are averse to cross-cultural themes. For example, in the Indiana Jones movies, Indy moves in and make friends from other cultures and has an interesting, adventuresome life. *See* Resources for video suggestions.

Story time. For bedtime stories, Gretchen Lovingood went to the library and found positive stories from other countries. "I picked stories where the children were close to our children's ages. After the story, I'd talk about poverty a little bit. I'd say, 'There are some people in the United States who have more money, but in this country there are a lot of people who are very poor.'

"It works better to have the child see another child who thinks and feels as they do. They feel empathy, yet equality with that child." (Mennonite Central Committee's videos in "Child's View Series" show how children in different parts of the world live. *See* Resources.) In talking about such stories, point out details like the games the children play, what the schools are like, toys the children enjoy.

Be on the lookout for stories of justice, love, and peacemaking. For example, Dr. Seuss books offer empathetic themes. *The Sneetches* tackles prejudice when the Sneetches question who's better: star-bellied sneetches or plain-bellied ones. In *Horton Hears a Who,* Horton cares about creatures too small to matter and insists they have as much right to live as bigger folks. My kids' favorite book when they were preschoolers was *The Digging-est Dog,* by Al Perkins, which illustrates that no one is hopeless. The dog is redeemed from the store, makes a mistake, but is forgiven and restored.

Gift Giving

It's hard to buy presents for most Americans. We have everything we really need and most of what we want. Let kids use a gift catalog such as the one from Alternative Gifts. These gifts offer basic necessities of life for others instead of items we quickly consume or leave unused. For example, my teenagers gave me an "alternative gift" on my birth-day—a solar cooker for a refugee camp in Kenya. Having a solar cooker meant that these East Africans could stop using stoves fueled by cow dung, which is full of parasites and germs—the cause of some of those thirty-five thousand deaths a day from preventable diseases.

Above my desk hangs a beautiful card from another alternative gift I received. The card explains that my kids gave money to replenish the tropical rain forest in Nicaragua. I cried as I read this, thinking about how our first sponsored child, a four-year-old girl, had been forced to flee Nicaragua with her family many years ago. They later returned, and this little girl is all grown up now. Maybe she can even see this growing rain forest. A gift with that kind of long-term meaning is much better than one more cookbook!

Many organizations offer practical ideas for groups that want to try alternative gift giving. For example, one Christmas Michael and Virginia Hostetler's extended family responded to an organization that provides school kits for children in developing nations. It's difficult for these kids to stay in school for lack of clothing and school supplies. The entire Hostetler family decided that instead of exchanging gifts, they would spend their money on notebooks, rulers, crayons, and pencils to make forty or fifty school kits. On Christmas Day, kids and adults formed an assembly line, producing nearly fifty bags and having a great time. (The Mennonite Central Committee offers a video about this program. *See* Resources.)

It is possible to care for people in great need and find joyful satisfaction at the same time. One word of caution from a friend (who is a grandma): She suggests that if you give such an alternative gift to a child, give the child something "fun and tangible," too. It's one more way to say that God loves you—*and* God loves this world.

QUESTIONS FOR CONSIDERATION

Choose a few of the following questions to discuss with others or to ponder yourself.

1. Imagine spending a day with the children in your life and doing a few things that immerse you and them in a culture other than your own (for example, eating out, reading a book, watching a video, going to a cultural festival). What would it look like?

2. Bring a blank postcard and ask members of the group to order the different gift catalogs mentioned in Resources under Gift Giving. Which one sounds most interesting to you?

3. If you were to do a "famine meal" with the children in your life, what would make it work? What would make it fail?

PERSONAL DEVOTIONS

May God be gracious to us and bless us and make his face to shine upon us, that your way may be known upon earth, your saving power among all nations. Let the peoples praise you, O God; let all the peoples praise you. Let the nations be glad and sing for joy, for you judge the peoples with equity and guide the nations upon earth.

—Psalm 67:1-4

PRAYER. I confess, O God, that I get confused by languages and customs I don't understand. Help me to enjoy the kaleidoscope of cultures you have put here on earth. Help me to enjoy their stories and their foods. Help me to model this for the children in my life. Amen.

Giving Voice to Empathy

When God's worldwide purposes weave themselves through our conversations and leisure moments, compassion becomes a natural response to life. When your kids are assigned social studies, language, or reading projects at school, they may look at you and say, "What was it you were saying about . . .?" (That's why it's good to keep those newspaper clippings!) Even if kids don't inquire about world issues, you can steer them toward research topics that move them beyond our own culture. Here are some ideas.

Book reports. When your child is required to report on a book, why not explore poets and writers from other cultures? Or choose books that revolve around biblical themes of justice and mercy. For example, the classic book *Cry, the Beloved Country* deals with issues of apartheid in South Africa in a powerful way. After reading it, you might rent the exceptional video that is now available and point out that author Alan Paton was quite a hero himself, resembling the deceased man in the novel who did so much to break down barriers.

World language classes. If your kids are learning a world language in school, ask them to teach you phrases that would help you be more friendly in another culture—something simple such as "Vaya con Dios" (Spanish for "Go with

God"). Be alert for ways this world language might come in handy. Maybe your church is sending a mission team to a country where that language is spoken or a day-care center needs a teen who speaks that language to work there.

Challenge kids to take an "other culture" slant on social studies projects. Kids often adopt the first viewpoint they hear, so it's important for parents to encourage them to keep an open mind. Sara Shenk tells about her son's research project on the Mexican-American War. "Everything he read made it sound like Mexico was stupid to put up resistance. He thought it would have been better for Mexico to have acquiesced. When my husband heard this, he urged him to dig a bit more and not view it from such a biased, U.S. perspective. He asked him, 'What did it look like from the Mexican side of things?'"

Son and father worked on the project together, showing how Mexicans viewed the United States as the aggressor and how the Mexican economy was devastated for years. "No one had written anything like this before, but he'd gotten all his information from familiar sources," says Sara. "He got an A+ on the paper."

The point is not to become bashers of the United States but to be empathetic Christians. To "love enemies" means to understand that opponents have viewpoints and desires that should be respected. Kids who believe

> Prayer reminds us that we're a part of the "family business" of blessing the families of the earth. We're partners in Christ's global cause.

their view is always right and the other person's view is always flawed have trouble being compassionate toward others. Even when people on the other side are clearly wrong, it's important to empathize with the terror and devastation they may have experienced in a conflict. "But they deserved it!" is not the view of those who are called to "lay down our lives for one another" (1 John 3:16).

Voicing an Opinion

Every family voices a complaint now and then—usually about a used car or a neighbor's barking dog. Justice seems like a big issue at these moments—justice for *me*! Biblical justice flows out of the prayer "Let my heart be broken by the things that break the heart of God." As those who "loose the bonds of injustice" (Isa. 58:6), we may turn our hearts toward others and write simple letters of complaint about situations that are unjust toward others.

Letters to Congress. Children can be involved in writing letters to congressional representatives supporting bills related to hunger relief and assistance to poor countries. Maybe this kind of letter writing seems unnecessary to you because you've heard about all the foreign aid the United States gives away. It might surprise you to know that one-third of this foreign aid is military and security aid. Do poor nations need more tanks and bullets, or do they need help to become agriculturally and economically stable? "Aid has been heavily concentrated in countries where the United States has strong political or security interests . . . [such as] Egypt and Israel."[1] When U.S. foreign aid plays to those priorities, it's more likely—not less likely—that thirty-five thousand children will die each day from preventable diseases.

Government leaders pay attention to issues they receive mail about, often limited to controversial issues. As it stands now, they receive much more mail in an average year about abortion (a political hot potato) than about hunger, yet "starving children and street kids far outnumber aborted babies in an average year."[2]

Letters to corporations. You've probably been stopped in front of a department store to sign a political petition. Although kids usually can't sign because they're not registered voters, you can invite them to sign other types of letters or petitions. The McGinnis family did this when they boycotted a well-known food company's products. For many years, this company has promoted the sale of infant formula to women in developing countries.[3] The use of formula has caused illness and death, because the water supply (with which the formula is mixed) is often not pure. When the McGinnis family wrote their letter to the corporation executives, they talked to their children about the issues and invited them to sign the letter as well.

Some of these discussions took a lot of time. One child thought that the formula was in this company's candy bars and that's why the family boycotted them![4] Thoughtful processing is important in an age of sound bites. If a child says no, that's OK too. We need to respect their opinions, but still invite them to join us.

Praying Together

Speaking of complaining, pleas for justice can be offered to God. In whatever settings your family prays, take time to turn the family's hearts toward others. This includes pleas for justice and also requests for mercy for "those whose work is dangerous: those whose work is monotonous . . .: those who can find no work to do."[5]

Table graces can routinely include places of conflict in the world. From a family that uses *Global Prayer Digest (GPD)* at the dinner table, one parent reports that reading the day's entry takes three and a half minutes. "I explain any difficult words to the children. . . . Then we pray for unreached people, groups, and missionaries."[6] Some families even collect loose change in a jar on the table and send it once a month to a mission agency. Now and then, *GPD* reports answers to prayer, which can be empowering to a family who has prayed for a nation.

Prayer reminds us that we're a part of the "family business" of blessing the families of the earth. We're partners in Christ's global cause: preaching good news, proclaiming freedom for prisoners, releasing the oppressed (Luke 4:18, 19). Missionaries have told me that prayers are important to them: "To pray for us is to be on the front lines."

I like praying for leaders in developing countries. I ask God to give them wisdom about spending government money on vaccinations and clean water to reduce that thirty-five-thousand–dying-kids-a-day statistic. I pray for the integrity of national leaders. It must be so difficult for people in power not to become concerned with amassing more power or money.

The Voice of Dollars

One of the most effective ways to voice empathy is through donating money. Jim McGinnis explains: "It's tough to ask children to give if you don't. Children have to see us give, and we have to talk to them about how we give."

For a year, the McGinnises gathered letters requesting funds, saved some that were interesting, and sat down at dinner to talk. (Their children were ten, twelve, and fourteen.) Jim and Kathy said to their kids, "Here are the ones that are asking for help. Which ones should we send money to?" and "We're going to give ___ dollars every quarter. Do you want to kick in some too?" The kids decided to help. Jim says, "The kids were free to bring different needs or causes from their life— something from school, something they read about in the paper."

By choosing to whom and what to give, the McGinnis children got to practice more of the Holocaust rescuers' skills: "cooperating and being responsible to promote the well-being of others" and being a part of a "group who valued compassion so there was not a sense of being in a struggle alone." These activities weren't weird or unusual, just normal behaviors of an adventuresome, caring family.

CHAPTER TEN

QUESTIONS FOR CONSIDERATION

Choose a few of the following questions to discuss with others or to
ponder yourself.

1. Which scenario, if any, can you see your family putting into
   action?
   • using a book such as *Cry, the Beloved Country* for a book
     report
   • taking the "other culture" slant on a social studies project
     (such as the Mexicans' view of the Mexican-American War)
   • writing letters to Congress members to support foreign aid
   • writing letters to a big corporation (like the McGinnises)
   • praying together for other nations
   • reading fundraising request letters and planning how to give

2. If your family were to do a joint giving project, how would it
   work best? How would you choose as a family? How would
   each family member contribute somehow?

PERSONAL DEVOTIONS

*Speak out for those who cannot speak, for the rights of all the
destitute. Speak out, judge righteously, defend the rights of the
poor and needy.*
                                                    —Proverbs 31:8-9

Imagine yourself speaking out for a voiceless person or group of
people. What does that look like? Are you writing a letter? organizing
a group? informing yourself for thoughtful conversations? writing a
gripping novel? speaking before a group?

PRAYER. O God, you have commanded us to speak out for those who
cannot speak. Show me how to do that. Show me how to do that with
grace and clarity and hope. Amen.

Volunteering as a Family

P erhaps you read the title of this chapter and thought, Volunteer as a family? Every parent has just fifty-two Saturdays! What does she expect?

Consider this: You probably already serve in several ways. What if you altered the ways you serve, so that you and your children serve together? This shift would accomplish many things at once. First, when families serve together, parents teach compassion by creating opportunities for them to serve. Next, serving together gives families quality (and often fun) time to spend together. Third, it relieves guilt. Parents no longer have to feel torn between family and church work. You don't have to run off and leave your kids one more night (and then feel so guilty that you resign from everything). Fourth, kids are more likely to stick with an avenue of service if they volunteer beside a parent or grandparent. Volunteering within the context of their family gives kids the security they need to reach out to others.

There actually is research to support that statement. A study by the Points of Light Foundation on family volunteerism found that as volunteers, families are more committed. They enjoy themselves more, since they're together, and they're likely to volunteer more frequently than individuals.[1]

That's not to say that every organization knows what to do with an entire family. When I called the volunteer coordinator at a downtown rescue mission to volunteer my family, she was stunned by my offer. We wanted to serve at a "neighborhood picnic" on the Fourth of July just after the Los Angeles riots. "We've never had a whole family volunteer before," she said. "This is so unusual. Your family can join the college group that's coming." And we did.

As anyone might guess, our eleven- and twelve-year-old children worked harder that day than they had ever worked in *my* kitchen. They cleaned up spills and cooperated with each other (gasp!) without one hint from Dad or me. I didn't growl when they accidentally splashed red punch on our white shirts. The four of us worked side by side, listening to guests' stories and holding undernourished, cooing babies. When one of us got tired, another spelled that one. Afterward we explored the crumbling walls of the mission. Just when we thought we were leaving, the kitchen help sat our two kids on stools and gave them huge tubs of ice cream. It was a special day in the life of our family.

What Can Kids Do?

The main roadblock to family volunteerism, according to the Points of Light study, is finding projects suitable for volunteer families. It's true that not every volunteer situation works for kids. If you're a grandparent, not every opportunity is doable for you. Find activities that are within the capabilities of all family members. *How a family serves together will be as different as families are themselves.*

You don't have to figure it all out for yourself. If you know another family that's volunteered together, ask them to tell your whole family about it. Then come up with several ideas, let the kids talk about it and choose. You might decide your family will serve in some way once a month. Keep a list of ideas going. Each month, your family can choose the activity together. Plan around regular activities and encourage kids to bring friends along, if you like. Of course, mix in fun activities too. Consider the following ideas.

Volunteering as a Family

Help with kids. Is there a church in town with a latchkey program or a summer "sidewalk Sunday school"? Perhaps it needs help. You and your kids can do simple things like serve refreshments. If you have a sponsored child overseas, you can pack a gift box for that child. (Check first with the sponsoring agency.)

Rachel Miller tells how she and her sons baby-sat at a transition home for new teenage mothers. What did she tell her sons about these unwed mothers? "My sons asked, 'Where are the dads?' and I had to explain some of the realities of teenage hormones. This led to conversations about them as boys and their responsibilities to deal with their hormones."

Serve a holiday dinner at a street mission. The simplicity and gratefulness exhibited at a holiday mission meal keep our celebrations in perspective. Our whole family served a Thanksgiving meal when our kids were preschoolers, and it was a fun day.

Bring a meal to a homebound elderly person. You can do this through a program such as Meals on Wheels or simply by adopting a senior citizen in your church as a "grandparent."

Invite international students to share a meal with you. International students who attend U.S. universities and small colleges are often lonely, especially when schools close during holidays. They may not even understand what U.S. holidays are about. Contact the student affairs office at a local college for names of students who need a place to go. International students may be more comfortable if two of them can go together. When students visit in your home, use the time to get to know them as individuals and learn about their culture.

International students often need conversation partners to help them learn English and customs, which means your family could develop an ongoing relationship with one or more. Many students need help with practical matters like getting a driver's license. Time spent with these students may have untold results—40 percent of the

Volunteering within the context of their family gives kids the security they need to reach out to others.

world's two hundred twenty heads of state once studied in the U.S., says International Students, Inc.[2] The church and Christian influence can make a world of difference in the lives of these future leaders. Contact International Students, Inc., for more information and to help with this effort. (*See* Resources.)

What if international students ask you questions about your faith? Wise missionaries have found that "a consistently Christ-like life is the most important factor in sharing the gospel."[3] Answer questions, but stay away from anything that smacks of superiority. Be respectful of their religion and offer to pray for them. People from nearly every world religion welcome prayers.

Having international students in your home is especially good for younger children who feel more comfortable serving in their own home environment. Give these little ones special jobs to do, questions to ask, or a simple game to teach the student.

Do be careful about embracing too many ideas that bring people into your home. Before overbooking, consider whether you will interfere with time when your children need attention. Is this activity something they want to do? Are they uncomfortable in a way they cannot articulate? You need to hear their heart. Is the activity a good idea but the time not right?

Do construction or maintenance outdoor projects. Many environmental organizations need help collecting trash or clearing brush. Join a group within your church that's cleaning an elderly person's yard. We once wanted to volunteer with Habitat for Humanity but had trouble figuring out how our kids would fit in. I finally found a Habitat chapter (not the closest one to us) that let us bring our kids who were then under sixteen.

Visit the sick. Just as Mary Price prepared her kids for a visit to the nursing home, Rachel Miller prepared her sons to meet her buddy in the Lancaster AIDS project (befriending someone with AIDS). She told them, "What you're going to see will be hard. The smell will be bad, and Rosie [Rachel's buddy] will look like a Holocaust survivor. I don't know if she'll be able to talk. You might feel awkward, but if you give her a hug and big smile, that will help her. If you find you can't handle it, that's OK. Wait for me in the car."

Being a buddy to an AIDS patient meant that Rachel was his or her friend until the person died. Rachel's sons have known all four of her buddies and visited them with her. "We've been in each other's homes for meals. We've gone shopping and played games. If they're in the hospital, we visit them there. My sons are learning that you can't take away pain and sadness, but you can help people by being a friend through it."

How does Rachel, a single parent who works full time, have time for this? "I've explained to my sons that I've made this choice, and I don't know how I'm going to squeeze it in. Yet I need to do this. Even when I don't enjoy certain times with my buddies, I know it's good for me. I want my sons to know it's a two-way street—both parties are helped."

How to Make Volunteering Work

Pray with your family ahead of time for the people you're going to serve. Let your kids see that your relationship with God motivates you to love others, that you are grateful for God's love and want to share it.

Look for opportunities that promote personal relationships. James McGinnis of the Parenting for Peace and Justice Network offers this wise counsel: "The key to a successful service project is the presence of a personal relationship that can motivate us to loving and sacrificial action for the long haul. Visits to a nursing home, homeless shelter or soup kitchen should have as their goal the development of a friendship with one of the residents. Friendships are more mutual experiences, and service means 'doing with' more than 'doing for.'"[4]

If you're spending Thanksgiving Day serving a dinner and your children are little, arrange for your kids to play with the guests' kids. If you want to develop a relationship with an international student, ask the same student to come again.

Serving side by side with our children brings all kinds of benefits to them too. They gain self-confidence as they see that they can make a difference in this world (with a parent alongside to assist when they goof). We're showing that we value them. They feel proud that we've invited them into our adult world to be of use to others. Later, with peers in other circumstances, they're more likely to emerge as leaders because they're used to helping, and they're not intimidated by someone who looks different or talks differently.

Most of all, our children are likely to become the kind of people who automatically pitch in, who naturally help the older person find a seat, because they've already done that kind of thing under our direction. From practice with us, they know to care for others, to share their time and possessions, to think about how the other person feels.[5] How's that for accomplishing several things with just a little effort?

QUESTIONS FOR CONSIDERATION

Choose a few of the following questions to discuss with others or to ponder yourself.

1. Which of these benefits of serving together would help your family?
    *   teaching compassion
    *   having quality time together

- relieving your guilt—you are serving God without neglecting the children in your life
- your children have a greater chance of becoming service-oriented adults

2. Which of these volunteer activities might you and the children in your life do together?

❑ helping with kids
❑ serving a holiday dinner at a street mission
❑ bringing a meal to a homebound elderly person
❑ inviting international students to share a meal
❑ doing construction or maintenance outdoor projects
❑ visiting the sick

PERSONAL DEVOTIONS

Two are better than one, because they have a good reward for their toil. For if they fall, one will lift up the other; but woe to one who is alone and falls and does not have another to help. Again, if two lie together, they keep warm; but how can one keep warm alone? And though one might prevail against another, two will withstand one. A threefold cord is not quickly broken.
—Ecclesiastes 4:9-12

Picture yourself and the children in your life as that threefold cord. When you serve alongside one another, how will they be stronger—in that moment and in their life?

PRAYER. Caring, eternal God, show me how to serve alongside my children with respect. Help them to become stronger because we serve together. Please help me to be fun. Amen.

CHAPTER ELEVEN

FAMILY DEVOTIONS

Read the verse above (or have children read it). Hold three pieces of twine in your hand and braid them. Explain that work *can seem* easier when we work alongside one another. It ends up looking better—more artful—like the braided twine, because more people contribute.

PRAYER. Thank you for families. Show us how to help one another and to enjoy being together as we work alongside one another.

Firsthand Cross-Cultural Experiences

I don't like to inconvenience parents, but this chapter includes some ideas that will ask you to go out of your way. On the other hand, I can't apologize for these suggestions, because providing firsthand cross-cultural experiences for children and grandchildren is worth the time, money, and effort. Such experiences make more of a difference than anything else you can do.

Why? Firsthand cross-cultural experiences foster relationships. When Doug Huneke evaluated what made the Holocaust rescuers empathetic and proactive, he found, "Friendship or familiarity with persons and cultures, with traditions and structures that are not a part of a person's usual set of life experiences, are essential. In 1979, a Louis Harris survey for the National Conference of Christians and Jews concluded that 'the most salient idea to emerge from the study is the fact that familiarity does not breed contempt. To the contrary, familiarity breeds acceptance and respect.'"[1]

Relationships change us. Most people remain entrenched in their prejudices, but the Holocaust rescuers had an "ability to confront and manage their prejudice." Why? The rescuers had experienced short-term acquaintances or long-term friendships with Jews before the oppression began.[2]

The McGinnis family saw how relationships change people when they traveled to Nicaragua and stayed with a family there. Jim observed, "There's nothing like that immersion experience in another culture to help children see that not everyone lives [like the folks on TV]." On their trip, then fifteen-year-old Theresa McGinnis bonded with thirteen-year-old Elizabeth, the daughter of the Nicaraguan family. Before they left, Elizabeth gave one of the two shirts she owned to Theresa as a present. Overwhelmed by Elizabeth's love and generosity, Theresa knew she could never match such a gift. But she pulled out of her suitcase one of the nine shirts she'd brought with her and gave it to Elizabeth anyway. Jim notes, "A kid remembers this forever."

Such exposure trips change the way you see God too. While covering a story in the Dominican Republic for a week, I discovered the rich experience of bonding with someone who looks and sounds nothing like me. Even though you don't speak each other's language well, you dress drastically differently, and you eat foods the other thinks are—let's say "strange"—there's a kinship. Jim McGinnis is right: that experience changes you forever.

If this wonderfully different person believes in Jesus Christ as you do, a "ping" goes off in your head that says: "God is real. Christ lives. Christianity wasn't invented by people at my church. God touches all people on this planet." You comprehend that God is not a glorified version of the brown-haired, average-looking white person portrayed in most drawings of Christ. You see that God is so intelligent, so diverse, so much bigger than you could ever imagine. That's such a healthy thing in this God-is-my-buddy world.

So let's look at various ways our children can have firsthand cross-cultural experiences.

In My Backyard

If you drew a circle with a ten-mile radius around your home, you might be surprised to find how many international people live there. *International children* are being adopted in the United States so frequently that it's no longer uncommon. If you have a friend or acquaintance who has adopted Romanian, Chinese, or Cherokee children and plans to educate them about their culture, you might ask if you and your kids could learn too.

Immigrant and refugee families do not settle only in big cities. In your neighborhood, you can probably find an Indian couple or a Middle Eastern young adult or an extended family of Cambodians. When you meet these families, remember the key for children to connect with others is playing together. Playing soccer was what bonded the Evans boys with the Hispanic kids.

Internationals have lived all around Jim and Barbara Hibschman in New Jersey for years. "We've tried to be openhearted to other cultures and religious backgrounds—Muslim, Buddhist, Hindu. We've invited them to join our family times, and our children participated in their home life. It's important to be a friend, to pronounce their names correctly."

When the Hibschmans and their church befriended a family of Hmong refugees from Vietnam, they helped them with their English. "We also helped them go to the grocery store and get a driver's license. We even went with them to take their birthing classes. That communicated to our children that we were cross-cultural people."

Visit other neighborhoods. Another sort of firsthand cross-cultural experience is to visit the inner city if you're suburbanites or rural areas if you're city dwellers. It's important to do this with an attitude of respect. Rachel Miller says that because she used to live in the "lily-white part of Lancaster County," she often took her sons into the city for festivals and concerts. "One of my sons went on a field trip to Philadelphia with his school, but it was like a 'zoo trip,' with kids saying, 'Gosh! Look at that!' I didn't want that. So before I took them to the city, I prepared them by talking about what it would be like to be homeless, especially how scary life can be on the streets. By advance discussions, we set ourselves up for a better, wholesome encounter."

Cross-Cultural Vacations

Many American families travel to other countries for vacations, but there's a difference between "well-traveled Americans" and "world Christians." The former, says missions pastor Paul Borthwick, "often act as though foreigners are their servants, that any inconvenience is intolerable, that beggars and lame people on the street are there to be photographed, and that other countries are subservient to or a subsidiary of the United States."[3] To avoid that attitude, it helps to be interested in the culture and an asker of questions. Here are some ways to do that.

Exposure vacations. Some organizations, such as Parenting for Peace and Justice, sponsor alternative family vacation and travel seminars. Ken and Gretchen Lovingood took their three grandchildren on one of these tours to Jamaica. Says Gretchen, "It was 50–50. We did social justice things and tourist things. Our eight-year-old grandson noticed they were driving on the 'wrong' side of the road. We told him, 'This is the *right* side here.' One of our teenagers wanted 'real' food. We teased her and said, 'This is real. To say this isn't real food is an insult.' That helped us explain to our grandchildren that things are different but not wrong."

The Lovingoods stayed with Jamaican families but also visited tin-roof shacks with no plumbing. Gretchen describes visiting a settlement house (or orphanage): "It was at the edge of a slum. As Danielle (our then fourteen-year-old granddaughter) walked by the nursery, she saw a baby crying and picked up the baby to hold it. She didn't care about his surroundings or even if she was supposed to pick him up. All she cared about was the fact that he cried and needed comfort. It was good to be able to talk about these experiences together."

Roots vacations. Although Blanca and Raul Castro were born in the United States, they wanted to take their kids to Puerto Rico, the nation of their heritage. Blanca thought, Let's do something that will stay in their minds and hearts for the rest of their lives. It will be expensive, but it will give them a defense against the materialism of America. That way, they'll never look down on someone who doesn't wear shoes.

The Castro kids now tell Blanca and Raul this was the best thing they could have done. Blanca says the families lived in two little bedrooms, "but that wasn't the big deal—it was the warmth and hospitality. There, the poor people live on ranches, and my kids loved seeing the cows run around. They enjoyed the simple life. They told me, 'Ma, this is so cool.'"

The Castro family also noticed that even though people were poor, they always offered them coffee and put out a table of food. "We thought about how here in America, people don't always offer you a glass of water—even though we have so much to spare."

Serving vacations. You can mix fun with a visit to a mission enterprise. Why? To "truly encounter the secrets of the land and its people is to serve them. By incorporating a short-term volunteer service or mission component into their vacation itinerary, 'travelers-in-service' can transform an ordinary excursion into a deeply meaningful travel adventure," wrote Dale Painter in *Discipleship Journal.*

Dale admits, however, that the thought of working or serving while on vacation was not always an appealing prospect! "At first I resisted the idea. After all, when I have a chance to 'get away from it all,' I want to relax, see the sights, and enjoy myself. If I want to work on my vacation, there are plenty of projects to be done at home!"

Still, Dale insists that vacation and service can be quite compatible. The Painter family spent part of their vacation on a Zuni reservation where they tutored students, assisted in janitorial projects, helped program computers, and wrote grant proposals. Dale said that "no AAA tour book could have led us into such an intriguing cultural experience," as he described being allowed to make the hike up a cliff to a sacred mesa and seeing ancient petroglyphs on the way. This is where "thousands of Zunis fled to escape the conquistadors. Today non-Zunis are forbidden to make this climb unless accompanied by someone from the reservation." Many such mission-oriented vacations offer insider information and moments not usually open to other visitors. Here are some guidelines Dale Painter offers:

1. *Decide what part of the country you'd like to visit.* Get out the maps. Fantasize. What about that dream to live with the Amish? Or places you've seen in travelogues or in *National Geographic?* Maybe it's a place you've already visited, but you long to experience it from the "inside."

2. *Take inventory of your skills, interests, and talents. . . .* Don't limit your assessment to your professional skills—often a change of pace from employment-related duties is important. Manual skills or interests in gardening, building, the outdoors, or writing may represent valuable resources to service organizations.

3. *[Decide how much of your vacation you're going to volunteer.]* Even service ventures that last only a few hours can produce meaningful experiences and be deeply appreciated.

4. *Evaluate how your children fit into your plans.* What projects can they get involved in? Which settings best appeal to their interests and sense of adventure? This is their vacation too, so be sensitive as you plan, and prepare them for a positive experience.

5. *Consider traveling with a local youth group as a driver or chaperon.* [This way] everything is already planned. All you need to do is follow along and participate. Often the experience will show you how easy it is to get involved and what a transforming experience such service can produce.

6. *Contact organizations that connect people with projects needing volunteers.*[4]

These guidelines can help you and your family dream a little. What would you and your family enjoy doing, if time and money weren't constraints? Talk with your family, dream a little more, and see what plans come of your dreams.

QUESTIONS FOR CONSIDERATION

Choose a few of the following questions to discuss with others or to ponder yourself.

1. Why do you think cross-cultural experiences and friendships have such a lasting impact on people?

2. Which of these ideas sound doable to you? (Check as many as you like.)

   ❑ befriending international children
   ❑ befriending immigrant and refugee families
   ❑ visiting other neighborhoods
   ❑ exposure vacations
   ❑ roots vacations
   ❑ serving vacations

3. Review the six guidelines for serving vacations at the end of the chapter. Which guideline would be most difficult for you? Why? Does the group have any ideas to help you?

PERSONAL DEVOTIONS

You shall also love the stranger, for you were strangers in the land of Egypt. You shall fear the Lord your God; him alone you shall worship; to him you shall hold fast, and by his name you shall swear. He is your praise; he is your God, who has done for you these great and awesome things that your own eyes have seen. Your ancestors went down to Egypt seventy persons; and now the Lord your God has made you as numerous as the stars in heaven.

—Deuteronomy 10:19-22

Consider the biblical concept of "the stranger." When have you welcomed a "stranger" (someone who is out of place for some reason) into your life and it turned out well?

PRAYER. You, O God, have commanded us to welcome strangers, even when it makes us uncomfortable. Give me the courage to venture out beyond my backyard and teach our children to do so as well. Amen.

Chapter Thirteen

Side by Side with the Church Community

W hen you're sure God's worldwide purposes are too big to be tackled by you and the children in your life, you're right. That's why God urges us to be in community with others. We need each other's support and knowhow. This was true of the Holocaust rescuers, one of the common traits being "development of a community of compassion and support." Rescuers who did not have this opportunity longed to share their work with others. "In those instances where groups of people or a whole community is engaged in rescue work, many more endangered people benefited."[1]

Working with others maximizes the benefits, because you share a common vision and affirm one another. It's one thing when *you* compliment your child on a napkin well folded; but let another adult do it, and kids love it! The work seems easier, because more people share the load and provide diverse skills. You don't know how to do a missionary newsletter, but you'd be glad to gather information. Spilling gallons of punch doesn't upset you so much when coworkers are laughing and helping you clean up. Community is, in fact, a key factor in avoiding burnout. You can often find community within an already established organization, which has some know-how.

The task of world missions is daunting, but

I've been encouraged by the pioneer missions movement. Research shows that people tend to evangelize their own culture group. That means a pioneer missionary's job is to penetrate each "people group," establish a beachhead, and then let indigenous missionaries work within that group. Accepting this model makes the task of world evangelization seem manageable and defines my role as praying for unreached people groups and giving to the cause.

Church as a Source of Community

Let's say you think helping the homeless in your area is too cumbersome for you and your family to tackle, that this task is best left to professionals. One of those professionals, Jan McDougall of Union Rescue Mission, disagrees. She cautions against believing that only professionals in inner-city missions are equipped to deal with problems of homelessness. She believes that the church is the highway around Skid Row. "A committed network of people who already know potentially homeless persons can help the most—before they get here."

The church makes a good highway for the flow of God's love, because we help one another when the task seems too overwhelming. Gerald and Sara Wenger Shenk's children have seen this close up. Sara relates how a man in their inner-city church struggled with alcoholism and drug addiction. "On good days, he was winsome and participated in church on the front row. On bad days, he slept on the street. We would lose track of him; but then he would call, and we would talk to him and pray for him at the table. He improved, then he regressed. The kids asked, 'Why can't he just get his act together?' We explained about the dark force of addiction, that he didn't know what it was to be loved. We were in a process of reparenting him."

The Shenks weren't the only ones helping him though. A lot of church members were involved with him too. "Finally, we all said there was no more we could do. Then he saw he had run out of good graces and agreed to be admitted to a rehabilitation program. He's doing well there now. It looks as if the work we invested and prayer may pay off. Each of us can give something but not everything."

Churches also provide an excellent place to serve with your children or grandchildren, because churches are often child-oriented. It's more likely kids can get involved with you in that setting than in some others. Here are some ideas for serving with your family through the local church.

Helping Missionaries

When missionaries visit your church, invite them to your home to eat a meal. Contact your pastor ahead of time, because missionaries' schedules are often hectic. Think of questions your children can ask them. Most of all, have fun. One adult missionary remembers: "I have vivid childhood memories of having missionaries to dinner. I learned they laughed at jokes and liked mashed potatoes—just like me!"[2]

If a missionary is coming to stay for a while, help him or her find a car, a house or apartment, and furniture. If a missionary couple has kids, they'll need school and health care information as well as toys and bunk beds. You may even want them to stay at your house for a while. (We had a missionary family of six stay with us for several months, and we had such good times together that we kept our favorite board game unpacked in the center of the dining room table for quick fun while they were there.) Once a missionary returns to the field, you may want to serve as a stateside liaison or prayer partner. If so, ask your children to help you fold the missionary's newsletters and share the missionary's news with your children.

As your children learn about letter writing in school, ask them to help you write letters to your church's missionaries. They can write about your family, pets, church, and even current events—especially details about the World Series or Superbowl! Be sure they ask the missionaries questions too: What does your home look like? What is your average day like? Do you have pets? Do you have plants or a garden? What kind of food do you eat? Read the replies together, and then ask your children to draw a picture of what they think the missionary's home or country looks like.[3]

Keep several aerograms (special overseas airmail stationery) on hand. If you are using regular stationery and envelopes, be sure to check on the correct postage (1-800-275-8777). You can send birthday cards to missionary kids, including stickers in the envelope.[4] Another idea is to tape record your message and send the cassette. Older kids may want to E-mail missionaries themselves.

If you'd like to send care packages, consider sending magazines you subscribe to that the missionaries would enjoy, such as *National Geographic* or *Guideposts*. Missionaries love, but rarely get, food parcels from home. This is especially true for first-time missionaries with kids who crave convenience foods that can be bought only at home. For more ideas, see the booklet *52 Fun Things Your Family Can Do Together for Missions* listed in Resources.

Missions Emphasis Moments

If your church has a missions emphasis Sunday or conference, make sure the kids don't get overlooked. Barbara Hibschman believes the key to presenting missions to kids is using materials and activities that appeal to all five senses, especially slides, videos, foods, games, and folk dances. "Once I had clothes from Ecuador the children could try on. I also included foods they could taste and curios they could touch. (I have a room full of 'jungle junk' I've collected at garage sales for such occasions.)" Barbara also uses tapes of music from the featured country, which she finds in the public library. Occasionally, she has found musical instruments from that land for the children to play.

The year Barbara featured Mexico, she allowed her daughter (who is fair and blond) to dye her hair dark to look like a Mexican girl! "I also allowed her to wear makeup, which surprised her because she was only ten. We dressed her up and she learned a few Spanish phrases." The missionary conference became the highlight of the year in the

Hibschman family—they knew Mom would let them do otherwise forbidden things at this time!

After a few years of Barbara's efforts, other parents got into the action, because they could see how the kids liked it. "One year a parent built an African hut where the children went to hear the missionary tell stories. Another time we decorated the room like Thailand, and the missionary dressed in Thai clothes, and we served Thai tea."

Youth Groups Serving

If your church has an active youth group, encourage the person in charge to consider mission trips. Laura Price went on a mission trip with her youth group to a Navajo reservation in New Mexico. There, they led a Vacation Bible School and did other service activities. It was a relationship-building event. Although Laura was in charge of activities, the thing she remembers most was sharing a moment with Molina, a Navajo girl, as they watched a bald eagle flying.

Laura was especially shocked the Navajos didn't have to lock their church buildings. "We lock our church buildings, but they leave them open to be used, because they're more respectful of churches. The girls slept upstairs in the church, and the guys slept downstairs. We got scared one night because we heard someone come in and use the bathroom. But this was normal. It's OK, not like here."

Many opportunities exist for youth groups to go on mission trips, especially for projects such as building homes in Appalachia or Tijuana, Mexico. You may want to do some legwork yourself, checking out various mission organizations. According to Kevin Johnson, advisor to youth pastors and author of *Catch the Wave,* look for trips that: consider legitimate safety concerns; make sure youths' time is spent making a difference (not perfecting a tan); provide clear information (are passports and shots needed?); include personal elements such as linking up with local Christians. It's also helpful to get the inside scoop from someone who has gone before on such a trip.

Youth groups can also do one-time events such as World Vision's "30

Hour Famine," usually held on Palm Sunday weekend. During that event, youth fast for thirty hours, learn about world poverty, and have a lot of fun. If you as a parent like such ideas, mention them to the youth pastor and offer to help.

Youth groups have also sponsored "hunger banquets." Invite a large group to the church and divide the participants by continents. Serve food according to the continent's access to food. Todd Evans explains how it works: "Those representing the United States get eighty cookies while all of Asia gets four cookies. We've also done this with whole meals. Some people get pork chops; others get only bread. The adults play along, but the kids usually don't stand for it." More specific ideas can be obtained from Parenting for Peace and Justice Network. (*See* Resources.)

In whatever way you serve, community is essential. You need to know you're not alone. One day when I learned that a longtime client at the Samaritan Center was pregnant *again* (she'd lost custody of all her other children), I got upset. I went to the kitchen and talked with another volunteer. She told me about the paperwork she was doing to get prenatal care for this woman. We both cried, and then I dusted myself off and went back to work at the shower desk. Having a pal to cry with, rail with, and laugh with makes all the difference.

QUESTIONS FOR CONSIDERATION

Choose a few of the following questions to discuss with others or to ponder yourself.

1. What are the advantages of serving with your church?

2. Kids love to be complimented by adults on their work by adults, especially in front of their parents. Why do you think that is? Is it difficult for you to compliment another child in front of your own child?

3. How do you respond to Barbara Hibschman's ideas for making missions studies so much fun?

PERSONAL DEVOTIONS

Go therefore and make disciples of all nations, baptizing them in the name of the Father and of the Son and of the Holy Spirit, and teaching them to obey everything that I have commanded you. And remember, I am with you always, to the end of the age.
—Matthew 28:19-20

How do you respond to this verse? Many times we respond by thinking, It sounds too hard for me! And it is, but God can give us some small part to play.

PRAYER. Show me my part in the "family business" of making yourself known. Give me the courage, desire, and know-how to be useful in this. Amen.

Linking with a Child Overseas

L et's say I knew about an opportunity for your children to get to know a child over-seas who lives in an impoverished family, has little access to health care, and isn't going to be able to continue in school because books and clothes cost too much. The children in your life could write to that child and receive letters. They could gaze at that child's picture every day and pray for that child. Meanwhile, you could send a few dollars a month that would resolve most of the problems listed above. Would you be interested?

This is what happens with child sponsorship. You don't save the world, but your family can make a huge difference in one child's life. You can give a developing nation another potential adult citizen who is healthy, educated, and knows something of the heart of God. In the meantime, your children get to bond with someone whose life is completely different from theirs. They get a taste and touch of that child's world.

You've probably seen advertisements in magazines for agencies that sponsor children. Methods vary among these organizations, and it helps to examine their different philosophies (by requesting information, especially a copy of their mission statement), but the idea is similar. While parents usually spearhead this, many teens initiate it as well. When Laura Price attended a youth convention, she was challenged to sponsor a child through Compassion International. "So we sponsor a four-year-old named Fredlyn in Haiti. Stephanie, my little sister, writes to him. They offer trips where you can go. I want to go to meet him."

Building Empathy for Your Sponsored Child

Listen to the news with ears for your sponsored child. Having a sponsored child can change the way you listen to the news. The earthquake or hurricane or famine becomes personal—you know someone who could have lost her home or whose school was destroyed.

Child sponsorship puts a name and face on wars. Suppose you overhear that there's fighting in Peru, where your family has a sponsored child. You and your kids listen closely. You hear that the fighting is mostly in the interior jungle, so you go over to the world map on the wall and show them that your child is in Lima—away from the interior jungle. Your girl is safe for now, but perhaps you stand in front of that world map and pray for her anyway.

Note what your children and the sponsored child have in common. Our kids loved volleyball, and so did one of our sponsored children, so we wrote him about how they made fearless dives for the ball and got scraped up. "Do you do that too?" we asked him. It helps if your sponsored child is close in age to one of your own children (you can request this), because it's easier for the family to imagine how the sponsored child feels and acts.

Investigate their culture. If you know people from your child's country, talk to them about it. A Thai friend told us exactly how to pronounce the name of our sponsored boy in Bangkok. Her description of Thailand's hot, sticky climate made us wonder how this boy survived playing volleyball! She even told us about impoverished parents' selling their children into slavery, and she told us she was glad we were helping this family financially, so the parents wouldn't consider doing anything like that.

If you can't find someone from your sponsored child's country, look through books and encyclopedias or ask travel agencies for information. *National Geographic*, in particular, takes you to faraway places with pictures and interesting details. You can find information about a certain country in the *National Geographic Index* (National Geographic Society, 1989), a reference book found in most libraries. (Some back issues can be ordered by calling 800-638-4077.) Child sponsorship is, however, a relationship, not a school project. Facts and pictures are important inasmuch as they help us walk in the child's shoes.

> *Sponsoring a child gives you a greater sense of partnering with God in bringing good news to the poor.*

Translate events from our culture to theirs. Use the information you receive from the sponsoring company to make your sponsored child's world more real to your kids. For example, one of our sponsored child's chores is cleaning. "How would housecleaning be different in the mountains of Honduras?" I asked my kids. We talked about how she would have to haul water to the house, heat it, and then scrub— without cleanser.

Enhancing the Sponsorship Experience

The experience of child sponsorship becomes more worthwhile to your sponsored child and to your children, the more you invest in it. Here are some ideas.

Write to the child. By writing, you send a part of yourself. Most organizations provide sponsors with an initial letter from the children and an address for writing to them. Compassion International workers in the Dominican Republic reported that it wasn't uncommon for kids receiving letters from sponsors to run through the streets waving them around in pride and delight.

David and Rebecca Nielson and their two children, Amanda and Wesley, have sponsored several children. Rebecca feels strongly that these children need not only money, but "they also need to know you care. They need a letter in the mail. In some ways, sponsoring children is a harder responsibility than raising my own kids. My kids are here, but these kids are off in a different area of the world. I have no control over their world. I can do only so much."

What can you write about to this stranger? Here are some suggestions:

- List your kids' five greatest interests (baseball, drawing) and ask your sponsored child about those interests in future letters.
- Ask the child about a favorite Bible story.
- Have your own kids talk about their struggle to study hard in school. Say you're proud of your sponsored child's effort to get an education.
- Summarize what's going in your family and send pictures, if possible, of new babies or new pets.
- Let your child know he or she is special. For example, describe for your sponsored child the setting in which your family reads his or her letter aloud.
- Ask the child about the materials used for activities (drawing, playing basketball): "What kind of ball do you use? How old is it?"
- Tell how your country looks compared to your child's country. For example, "My state is dry and desert like, but I hear that your country has a lot of green hills."

Pray with your kids for your sponsored child. Whenever you routinely pray with your children, pray for your sponsored child. We've always included our sponsored child in our dinner table grace. Pray for the child's walk with Christ; for safety from wars, recessions, and natural disasters; for health and physical growth and for health caregivers; for a full stomach when he or she goes to bed at night; for parents' health and employment; for education to continue in spite of obstacles.

Visit your sponsored child. If you'd like to take a vacation that is both fun and enlightening, sponsoring organizations often provide tours that visit your sponsored child as well as resorts in the area. Throughout the tour, you have a guide who knows the country. This way your vacation is about people and relationships, as well as seeing and doing new things.

The Nielson family took their two children to the Dominican Republic to meet two of their sponsored children. You may wonder why parents would spend all that money to take their children to an impoverished developing country instead of to Disneyland. Rebecca reflects, "We wanted our children to open their hearts, not to look down on those less fortunate. We wanted to involve them in the sponsorship process, so that the pictures on the refrigerator were real people to them."

Rebecca says the trip was also a reality check for herself—she needed to see how the rest of the world lives. Their family descended upon the crowded, littered streets of this hot Caribbean country, which looked very different from their neighborhood in the well-fed snow belt of northern Michigan. Amanda (then thirteen years old) thought conditions were worse than what she'd ever seen in America. "At one place, seven people lived in one room, and the wooden floor was caving in. They didn't have garbage dumps, so the garbage sat around. There was broken glass all over, and little kids ran around without shoes and cut their feet." Amanda also noticed that the kids there were smaller than in America. "I guess because they're malnourished. Kids who were six were the same height as my cousin who is three. Even the dogs were skinny! Most places have malls, right? I never saw one."

Rebecca's son, Wesley, who was ten at the time, was stunned by the schools: "All ages were in one room. They didn't have desks to put stuff in, just tables and chairs. In the market, chickens hung on hooks with flies on them. But their houses were really clean. When you think about poor people, you think things will be messy and junky, but they weren't. They had no electricity—you wonder how they cleaned things. It's crowded there too. There was no place to get away. I have a tree that I go up and climb and can be alone, and I can think. I wish they had that."

After the family met their sponsored children, Mauricio and Jeanny, the whole group went to a pizza parlor. There, a translator helped the Nielson family ask the two children questions about their homes. Some of their answers were confusing as they spoke of having televisions, inside bathrooms, and running water. This confused the Nielsons until a Compassion International worker took them aside to explain that sponsored children sometimes stretch the truth in order to impress their sponsors. They want to be liked by their American benefactors and even fear rejection.

Rather than being annoyed, the Nielsons were touched that these kids wanted their approval. "I saw myself in Jeanny," said Rebecca. "I wanted to be accepted at that age (fourteen). I wanted to put my arms around her and tell her it is OK not to have what other people have. When we finally touched heart to heart as we said good-bye, I could see it in her eyes."

As a vacation, this worked for the Nielsons. "Not only are you meeting your sponsored children, but you're getting away from all the things that drive our lives," relates David, who liked it that Mom and Dad weren't the boss! "The kids had to go along with the program. Whining about it didn't help—so there was a lot less of it."

Is it worth it to "waste" money on a trip when you could be spending it on the child? Most people agree that visiting a developing country changes you for life. You have concrete images in your mind: kids sharing beds, a home with cardboard walls, wires hanging from the ceiling with one light bulb powered by an extension cord stretched from another building. When you hear someone say that God supplies all our needs, you think a little harder about what that entails.

Sponsoring a child gives you a greater sense of partnering with God in bringing good news to the poor. It also makes God's global concerns more manageable, because there's one corner of the world where you're making a difference.

QUESTIONS FOR CONSIDERATION

Choose a few of the following questions to discuss with others or to ponder yourself.

1. If you had a sponsored child, what ways do you see yourself using to help your children connect with the sponsored child?

    ❑ investigating the sponsored child's culture
    ❑ writing to the sponsored child
    ❑ praying for the child
    ❑ visiting the child
    ❑ listening for news about that child's country
    ❑ noting what the child has in common with yours

2. If you were going to sponsor a child, what questions would you ask the child-sponsoring organization about how the child benefits from your monthly contribution (health, clothing, education, spiritual development, financial assistance to family, economic assistance to community, assistance in building infrastructure in the community)? about how the money is spent? about your involvement?

3. Monthly donations for child sponsorship typically are about $20–$25. What would your family have to give up to make that donation?

PERSONAL DEVOTIONS

Then little children were being brought to him in order that he might lay his hands on them and pray. The disciples spoke sternly to those who brought them; but Jesus said, "Let the little children come to me, and do not stop them; for it is to such as these that the kingdom of heaven belongs." And he laid his hands on them and went on his way.

—Matthew 19:13-15

PRAYER. Forgive me when helping one child does not seem significant enough to bother with. Help me to be like Jesus, who was good at seeing individuals and blessing them. Amen.

FAMILY DEVOTIONS

I was a father to the needy; I took up the case of the stranger.
—Job 29:16, NIV

Explain to your children that God puts those who are "strangers" in the same category as the "needy." Talk about the biblical concept of welcoming "the stranger." Ask them who the "strangers" are in their world—people who are out of place for some reason?

Or, you might want to use this time to tell about the Painters' visit to the Zuni reservation (*see* chapter 12).

PRAYER. Thank you, O God, for the sense of familiarity and home that we feel. Help us to welcome others who feel excluded. Amen.

chapter Fifteen

Shedding Stereotypes

Undoubtedly, the Holocaust rescuers as children heard many jokes and derisive comments about Jews. Yet they didn't let the generalizations behind these remarks erode their empathy. How did they withstand the subtle persuasiveness of this humor? Perhaps that morally articulate adult in their lives—a parent or grandparent—didn't make such jokes and didn't laugh when others did.

Shedding stereotypes is important for everyone's well-being, even for the groups who appear to dominate. The most difficult place to empty ourselves and "look . . . to the interests of others" (Phil. 2:4) is when we find ourselves in a power-up position. Can I refuse to use that advantage? Can I pass on being favored? Can I avoid letting skin color define who's in charge? If the group being discriminated against isn't my group, do I still care?

Since prejudice injures both the offender and offended, antagonism against the elderly, the disabled, and certain races hurts everyone and should be everyone's business. People tend to think that addressing racism, for example, is the task of minority folks— weren't African Americans the ones who brought it up anyway? It's their problem. Then white folks consider themselves magnanimously charitable anytime they're nice to an African American, Native American, Hispanic American. This attitude violates that golden and well-known rule of treating others as you would like to be treated.

They All Look Alike to Me

All the "isms" are subsets of lump-sum thinking, in which we see people in groups and categories, instead of as individuals with hearts that God is drawing. Some categorize immigrants as people grubbing for money, when they have no idea how desperately poor and politically dangerous life can be in other countries. Or all poor people are labeled lazy. When missionary couple Marc and Anita Hostetler came back to the United States, they fell on hard times and were forced to use food stamps temporarily. Anita told me, "People think that anybody on food stamps is lazy. We weren't lazy, we were just struggling. When people in the grocery store saw that we had food stamps, they treated us differently. The people behind us in line examined what we bought. One clerk said, 'Don't come back here again today with those food stamps.' They think poor people aren't entitled to some respect too."

People often stereotype prisoners and the newly released, concluding that being in prison makes a person a monster. I felt this prejudice keenly one day as my kids and I watched a fire spread through a nearby meadow. A bus with bars on the windows, filled with teenagers dressed to help fight the fire, pulled up. As they got out of the bus, some neighbor kids asked me who they were. I said, "A bunch of kids." The man next to me snickered and whispered, "Aren't you going to tell them who those kids *really* are?"

"After they've seen them in action," I replied. I wanted my kids to see these convicted teen felons work hard before I told the neighborhood kids that these teens were in jail. They deserved some credit before a negative label fell on their shoulders.

Lump-sum thinking is an equal-opportunity problem. Sharon Norris described her kids' reactions to white folks on TV. "My sons decided white folks can't control their children. They said that on television white parents always reason with their children and the children talk back to them. One time they said, 'You'd never let us get away with that. They should have a black mama!' So we talked about how parents of every race struggle to discipline their kids."

Sometimes we think lump-sum thinking is OK if the lump is bigger. If we put people in "our group," we give them more value. So we say things such as, "Love sees no color." No, loves sees color and is interested in that color's culture and that person's heart.

Bonding, relationships, even short acquaintances, disprove stereotypes. Missions pastor Paul Borthwick tells this story of students whose stereotypes faded in an afternoon.

A small group from our youth ministry went into Boston to enlarge our vision. The missionary who went with us had come from the suburbs, just like us, so he knew the stereotypes that filled our heads as we saw row houses, vacant lots, and the people of the city. Knowing the false impressions we had in mind, the missionary gave us . . . paper and pens and told us we had two hours to walk about the city. He instructed us to list all the things we observed that were different from our living situation and encouraged us to focus on aspects of the city that were better than where we lived in the suburbs.

At first, the students (and leaders, too) thought, *This won't take long.* To our surprise, we observed many positive things about the city. Students came back with long lists of observations like:

"Many people sit on their steps and talk to their neighbors; where I live, people are too busy to talk to their neighbors (if they even know their neighbors!)."

"People speak two or even more languages; I can only speak English."

"People don't have to worry about mowing their lawns."

"The stores are closer; you can live without a car."

"The neighbors all seemed to know each other. They told us that they protected each other. There was a sense of security and 'family' in their neighborhood, unlike mine."

CHAPTER FIFTEEN

"It wasn't like I pictured. I expected to see hookers and drug pushers. I'm sure they were there, but most of the people I met seemed pretty average, just like me."[1]

Just like me. Most people want the same things from life: friends, safety, health, acceptance, and a way to make a living.

Examine Our Own Stereotypes

Children do pick up prejudices from friends but mostly from parents when it "leaks" out of our mouths. Often we're unaware of our embedded ideas of who does and doesn't deserve things. To grow compassionate, empathetic children, we start by asking ourselves hard questions about our stereotypes. Assume no one could hear you, then complete these sentences: All Asians are _____. All blacks are _____. All disabled people are _____. All elderly people are _____.

Many people believe it's OK to be prejudiced if you're outnumbered or overwhelmed. For example, having one Korean family in your neighborhood is OK; but if the neighborhood "turned" Korean, you'd move. Or it's OK to talk to the disabled fellow at church, but to be friends who might go to an amusement park together—that would be a drag. That's why it's important to be diligent in weeding out our presuppositions.

As we explore prejudices, we can admit our failures to our children and thereby model "opportunities to examine prejudices," so important to Holocaust rescuers as children. "To develop broad egalitarian and humanitarian beliefs, and to instill respect for the pluralism of the world before judgments and stereotypes become ingrained are essential."[2] That's why we proactively challenge our kids with hypothetical neighborhood situations and say, "What would you do if . . . ?"

Shedding Stereotypes

Proactively Accepting and Caring

Here are some ideas for modeling openness and concern for all people God has created.

Respect others' cultures and beliefs. The average Westerner is appalled at people in Indian restaurants eating with their fingers. "Indians look at this differently," explains anthropology professor Paul Hiebert. "They wash their hands carefully and besides, when they see forks and spoons they see utensils that have already been in a lot of other people's mouths!"

We also criticize Indians for not killing and eating their cows to avoid hunger. Since they value humans and animals equally, they respond the same way we would respond if someone suggested we should shoot poor people to solve poverty in this country.[3]

Respect for others helps us see the irony of thinking our way is right or that some people actually have more rights to the park or park bench than others. I felt this irony intensely one day while standing in line at the post office several years ago. We're so worried about newcomers "taking over," when nearly every population have been newcomers "taking over" at some time. Two older white women in line were murmuring about the tragedy of our "changing community" (Inglewood, California), which had become predominantly African-American. A few feet from these women was a huge mural spanning the entire wall. The mural portrayed a scene from three hundred years before. Local Native Americans were showing European explorers the Centinela Springs, located just a few miles from the post office. I wanted to point to the mural and say, "If Indians could share with us, why can't we share too?"

I didn't. I decided that to speak up probably wouldn't influence those ladies much, but I would be "morally articulate" with my own kids. So I turned to my two children and we examined the mural together.

"When did white people come?" my kids asked as we looked at the mural. I threw out a few dates. Then I mentioned a much later date when my grandfather came to America from Germany. "Our family hasn't been here that long," I said. I told them how my grandfather could speak only German when he arrived. He did poorly in school because he understood nothing the first few years.

"Why didn't he go to an ESL class?" my son asked, referring to an English as a Second Language class. I laughed and explained that they didn't have those classes back then.

I began thinking about how I complained about newcomers who didn't know English. Did their parents insist, as my grandfather's did, that they only speak their native tongue at home? I had not considered these issues in this light before.

Don't eliminate the cross-cultural edge from scripture. Jesus had a habit of meeting or making a big deal out of the Jews' least favorite ethnic group, the Samaritans. He picked a Samaritan to be the hero of one of his wildest parables. Luke, the Gentile Gospel writer, was careful to mention that the one leper in ten that came back was a Samaritan.

What if you read these stories to your child or teenager and substituted *Samaritan* or *leper* with "Iraqi patriot" or "AIDS victim"? Ask them to imagine the fright of the poor beaten Jew waking up in the Holiday Inn to be told he'd been rescued by a Palestinian commando.

Justice and reconciliation themes are often overlooked. How many kids understand that Jonah ended up in the belly of the great fish because of his racial prejudice? Jonah didn't want Nineveh to be saved (Jon. 4:1-3) because as an Israelite, he despised this pagan, Gentile city. God obviously did not agree! In our age of ethnic cleansing, kids need to hear these stories in the context of their times—and ours.

Use respectful terms. While speaking with political correctness has had its excesses, it has also spurred me to consider how I can be more respectful. I asked several of my African-American friends how they felt about the terms *black* and *African American*. They all preferred the latter, so I use the term African American out of respect for my friends. I have a paraplegic friend who told me he prefers *disabled* over *handicapped.* I don't need a brilliant reason—it's enough to care for my friend. Isn't that what empathy is about—caring enough about people to use terms that help them?

Name prejudice for what it is. Mary Price told me, "Every time we read about a racial incident, we name it for what it is—racism. When we overhear racist comments, we refute them." Yet Mary seems to know how to do this in love. Their family's beloved Granny believes that people shouldn't marry outside their race, so often when she sees an interracial couple, she mentions it. Mary has walked a fine line of "refuting that but being loving and caring about it." Daughter Laura has picked up this ability from Mary. When Granny comments on interracial couples as she and Laura watch TV, Laura has also challenged her in a loving way.

One way to refute stereotypes is with information encased in those one-liners you pick up here and there. One I recently learned has stayed with me because I live in a state where immigration is a volatile issue: "Nearly half of African immigrants . . . have college degrees." Over the last thirty years, the United States has become home to the most highly educated newcomers ever to come to American shores.[4] That one-liner presents a picture very different from the immigrants-come-here-only-to-receive-welfare generalization.

Don't limit friends to one race. Your kids will catch on best if you invite friends of all races to your home. People may know one another at work, school, or church, but crossing one another's home thresholds is a key. Will I be comfortable at a party in their neighborhood? How will I feel if I'm the only white/African-American/Hispanic/Asian person? It's close-up interaction that brings respect and camaraderie.

Once when my son was small and some African-American friends were eating dinner with us, he and I caught each other peeking during grace. We were staring at the same thing—clutched hands around the table creating an ebony-and-ivory effect—black and white and black and white. His bright five-year-old eyes lit up and I winked. These are the kinds of experiences we don't want our kids to forget.

QUESTIONS FOR CONSIDERATION

Choose a few of the following questions to discuss with others or to ponder yourself.

1. Name one place or situation where you are in a power-up position and one place or situation you are in a power-down position. In what situations are the children in your life voiceless?

2. What has been helpful to you in combating the growth of racism in your children's attitudes?

3. If you have been enlightened by stories or insights from friends in another race or culture, share that with the group. (Examples from this chapter were the story about Indians thinking that eating with fingers is more sanitary than eating with forks and Sharon Norris's story about her sons' thinking white parents are permissive.)

PERSONAL DEVOTIONS

My brothers and sisters, do you with your acts of favoritism really believe in our glorious Lord Jesus Christ? . . . You do well if you really fulfill the royal law according to the scripture, "You shall love your neighbor as yourself." But if you show partiality, you commit sin.

—James 2:1, 8, 9

PRAYER. Forgive me for dismissing people or treating them as "less than" myself. Help me to love and respect others. Amen.

Handling Affluence

Most people, especially children, view life through the eyes of the culture— the way people around them automatically think, typically make choices, and normally behave. Part of our job is to see where the radical heart of Christ differs from the culture and gently remove the cultural glasses. Just for a moment, we want to present the reality of how our loving, just God designed things to work.

Part of the clarity we as parents provide is to examine the truth of the advertisements bombarding children. Various items, from hair dye to sneakers to lingerie, are purported to bring us self-worth, confidence, unlimited pleasure, and meaning in life. We can be loved, find joy, experience peace in life through these items. Says sociologist Tony Campolo, "The fruit of the spirit, suggests the media, can be had without God."[1]

Without being grumpy killjoys, we can point out how God provides for our deep emotional and psychological needs without the benefit of vast material goods. We ourselves must not be seduced. For birthdays and holidays, we need to convince ourselves that kids don't need ever-increasing quantities of stuff to be happy; anyone knows that a certain-age child can find great pleasure for at least a week with a huge empty box.

Simplicity Begins with Us

We have to live at the "need" level, not the "greed" level. When we look at the increase in size of the typical American house in the last forty years—more bedrooms, more closets, more garage space—we resemble the prosperous farmer who tore down his ample barns to build bigger ones (Luke 12:16-21). It would have been a radical idea to have given the extra away—just as it is with us.

When we let God transform our lust for bigger barns, we can bring our kids alongside in the following ways:

Present radical ideas. Help your kids "think like a hero to behave like a merely decent human being"[2] by presenting heroic, outrageous ideas now and then. For example, how would your kids (or you) feel about abiding by "National Buy Nothing Day" on the day after Thanksgiving? An organization named Adbusters challenges Americans to abstain from shopping on this biggest shopping day of the year. "Our goal is to galvanize resistance against those who would destroy the environment, pollute our minds and diminish our lives." In defense of Buy Nothing Day, Adbusters reminds us, "The average North American consumes five times more than a Mexican, ten times more than a Chinese person, and thirty times more than a person from India. . . . Give it a rest."[3]

Start by sending your kids to the Adbusters Web site (http://www.adbusters.org) to enjoy the funny spoof ads and thought-provoking design campaigns. This delightfully iconoclastic cyber hangout encourages us all to tread lightly on the planet, downshift our lifestyles, and lower the volume of our consumer culture's propaganda machine.

Even if your kids think your idea is strange or weird, discuss it. Remember how the Vogts brought up owning only one car? They weren't sure if they would actually do it, but just discussing it was a good idea. It helps kids "*think* like a hero" for a minute or two.

Recycle what you have. Most kids have too many toys and too many clothes. Instead of buying bigger storage containers and filling up more closet space, give things away. Keep a "give-away box" in the garage. Certain organizations pick up items monthly. You might want to be on such a list. When kids clean their room, put the give-away box prominently alongside the trash can.

Demythologizing the Simple Lifestyle

I like the statement "Live simply so that others may simply live," but I'm baffled about how to help my kids do that. Susan Vogt fleshed this out in an article titled, "Children, Money and Values: Ten Principles."[4] Here are her ten ideas, adapted and expanded with some additional thoughts from Susan and others.

1. Give allowances. "A modest amount of regular spending money can help the child learn the value of money and have the power to get things the parents might think are frivolous," notes Susan. "The children then learn their own lessons about what is worth buying without the parent preaching."

It's also good to teach children to give a portion of what they receive from that allowance and from their first jobs. You might suggest things that would be interesting for them to give to or issues they've become concerned about. My son is part of a youth group at a church in a nearby Hispanic neighborhood. We suggested he tithe there. He knew the needs, and it gave him a lot of joy.

2. Institute a clothing allowance. Susan Vogt emphasized: "When your kids get to an age

Simplicity begins with us. We have to live at the "need" level, not the "greed" level.

where they contest the reasonable and thrifty clothes you buy for them, give them a whole year's [clothing] allowance and let them decide whether to blow it on a couple pair of popular running shoes or rather to discover the joys of bargains and discount stores." The Vogts started this at different ages with each child. Their daughter Heidi began earlier than the others, because she was concerned about clothes. One son didn't care about clothes and never had such an allowance.

Heidi's response? "[The allowance] started at $100 and I wanted fourteen different outfits. (Only half of my shoes came out of the allowance.) I decided it wasn't large enough. So we wrote out a budget on an index card. At times, we made deals on special items. I wanted a $70 dress once. Mom said no. She said it wasn't just the money, but the principle of owning a dress that cost that much. The idea of not owning a dress based on principle was too wild for me! We worked out a deal."

Heidi also reported: "It's funny. When I was young, we went to Salvation Army stores and I said, 'No more. Only poor people go there!' But by the time I was a junior and senior, I liked to go there to get great deals."

3. *Seek a balance.* Susan says, "If parents are perceived as scrooges, children may resent having a thrifty lifestyle forced upon them and rebel to the opposite extreme. An occasional splurge is good for the soul and can let your kids know you're human. For example, although we don't typically buy expensive brand name clothes for our children, sometimes we've made an exception if it was a quality item, just to break our image as tightwads."

Kids want to know that you love them and want to take good care of them. One of Sara Wenger Shenk's sons wanted some famous name brand clothes and shoes because of peer pressure. They talked about it a lot, but she insisted on buying good quality, not famous name brands. After they finished the much-discussed shoe purchase, her son said to her, "I see now that you're not stingy but just careful." That made Sara glad. "He saw we had certain principles. We weren't guided by what culture says but whether it feels like a good use of the resources we have."

4. The simple lifestyle need not mean living in destitution, but it does mean that we must never be so isolated from the poor that we fail to be touched by their pain. Constant exposure to the poor can naturally motivate us to downsize our way of life. For example, the Vogt family chose to live in a lower middle-class, blue-collar neighborhood. They don't always go to the mall to shop. Instead, they often go to "a corner five-and-dime store that is rundown. Anytime we can get away from chains and franchises and patronize a mom-and-pop store, we do. At times, this means sacrificing time and convenience." Susan also took the kids to play in public areas in less affluent areas and sometimes went to a health clinic instead of a private doctor, especially for standard immunizations.

"We also take bike rides in neighborhoods that are different from ours—a lower socioeconomic neighborhood or a richer one. (Bike rides are better than walking because it takes away the temptation of gawking and feeling so out of place and awkward. On bikes, you can stop at a corner bakery or deli.) These rides raise questions: 'Why don't those people fix up their houses? Why is there so much litter?' That gives us openings to say, 'They don't have enough money to fix their homes.' So the kids ask why and we tell them, 'Because they don't have a job that makes good money.' Why? 'Because they didn't go to schools that were good. They didn't have parents that motivated them. Maybe the parents were sick or disabled. They were not given opportunities you have. They didn't have good connections.'" (When I interviewed the Vogts' daughter, Heidi, now twenty-two, and asked her about these bike rides, she was surprised to find out that's what the bike rides were about. She thought they were just riding to breakfast together as a family.)

The Simple Life Is Relational

Several of Susan Vogt's principles are based on relationships with people—often a forgotten factor in affluence.

5. People are more important than things. Susan decided that if the kid next door ruined one of her kids' shirts or video games, she would not make the kid next door feel bad. She urged her kids not to make a big deal about it either. Barbara Hibschman stressed to her kids that important decisions aren't made on money alone—even if you're an adult. "If you're offered a better paying job, that's not the only criterion that's important. How it affects people or relocates you is also very important."

6. *Hang around with people with [simple] values like yours.* "It's easier to say 'no' to a purchase when you can point out friends who have similar family standards," Susan reports.

7. *Gift-giving criteria.* "When you encourage the giving of gifts that are creative and may not cost money, the gift of one's effort and time are thus highlighted. Although we have done a lot of coupons for services and craft projects, we also found out the hard way that it's important to give at least one item that they can unwrap and might be considered a 'heart's desire.'"

Making the Simple Life Easier for Kids

8. *Start young.* "It's a lot easier to maintain a modest lifestyle if that's how the children have grown up. For example, if the policy at the grocery store has always been no trinkets, it's easier than backing off from trinkets later."

9. *Reduce temptation.* "Sometimes it can be so overwhelming that it's easier to just minimize the commercials seen by limiting TV and not spending much time in stores." When going in stores, it can help to make lists and stick to them or by shopping without children along.

10. *Make the "green movement" an ally.* Susan advises, "Although our kids sometimes think this 'simple lifestyle stuff' is pretty square, they can get into the school's emphasis on 'reduce, reuse, recycle.' Donate to the thrift store and then also go there for good buys."

QUESTIONS FOR CONSIDERATION

Choose a few of the following questions to discuss with others or to ponder yourself.

1. In what ways have you tried to communicate to your kids that people are more important than things?

2. How hard would it be for you to do the following yourself:

    Not shop on the day after Thanksgiving
    ❑ Very difficult
    ❑ Difficult
    ❑ Not difficult
    ❑ Easy

    Stick to a clothing allowance
    ❑ Very difficult
    ❑ Difficult
    ❑ Not difficult
    ❑ Easy

    Minimize your time shopping in stores
    ❑ Very difficult
    ❑ Difficult
    ❑ Not difficult
    ❑ Easy

3. What are you willing to do to reduce materialism and simplify your life?

PERSONAL DEVOTIONS

And [Jesus] said to them, "Take care! Be on your guard against all kinds of greed; for one's life does not consist in the abundance of possessions." Then he told them a parable: "The land of a rich man produced abundantly. And he thought to himself, 'What should I do, for I have no place to store my crops?' Then he said,

'I will do this: I will pull down my barns and build larger ones, and there I will store all my grain and my goods. And I will say to my soul, Soul, you have ample goods laid up for many years; relax, eat, drink, be merry.' But God said to him, 'You fool! This very night your life is being demanded of you. And the things you have prepared, whose will they be?' So it is with those who store up treasures for themselves but are not rich toward God."
—Luke 12:15-21

If you find yourself reluctant to give items away, why do you think that is?

PRAYER. Thank you, O God, for providing all that I need. Teach me to be content with what I have and to find satisfaction for my soul in you. Amen.

What You Can Expect to Happen

C ompassion is as much caught by kids as taught to kids. You can expect your children or grandchildren to catch your compassion if your heart is truly touched by God's worldwide purposes. In fact, your kids' compassion will surpass yours. They'll come up with ideas and ask you to match funds. Then the children in your life will model for you what you've modeled for them—a sense that God so loves me and so loves the world.

Are They Paying Attention?

You may be thinking, If I try these things, my kids will think I'm nuts! I've felt that way many times, which is why I asked Heidi Vogt, in looking back at her childhood, "Did this compassion stuff ever catch on? How did you handle the simple lifestyle?"

Heidi told me that as a kid, it *is* hard to understand. "All I knew was that we were different from the people around us. We kids saw *ourselves* as poor and oppressed because we didn't have a VCR for the longest time. This was not normal!

"It wasn't OK in our family to spend a lot of money on clothes or a car—the status markers that people see every day. When I was in high school, we had a dark green rusty '77 Celica. I was born in 1977! I hated to be picked up from school in it. When I called my dad to pick me up, I'd ask him what car he had. If he had the Celica, I'd finally say, 'OK, just come.'"

So far, Heidi sounded like my kids (who are younger than Heidi), but I kept listening: "I would suddenly get bursts of realization when I was walking somewhere with my dad and saw him stop and have a conversation with a guy asking for money. Sometimes he gave him money. When it was over, we'd say, 'Dad, did you know that guy?' 'No,' he'd say real loud. He was so intentional about helping people though. It impressed me so much. He'd say to them, 'How's it going? Can I get you anything?' We had a dinner table discussion about whether it makes sense to give money to panhandlers. My dad's attitude was, I've got more money than they do. They need it more than I do. But he never gave money just because somebody panhandled. He always talked and said hello."

At this writing, Heidi is leaving to work for the Peace Corps in Mali. I asked her why she was doing this. "It just sort of happened. During the summer of my junior year in college, I had an internship at a huge publishing house, but it all went back to the bottom line—money. They published high quality books on history, and I asked why they published what they published. They published only what people wanted to read and the pictures they'd want to see. The major goal was to create a profit, not to make important books. They didn't ask themselves what was important for people to know. I saw that important things can get lost in a company that prints wonderful books.

"So before I got a journalism job and entered the world of the office cubicle, I wanted to go somewhere where I could experience a different reality of life. I'm going to the Peace Corps, because I want to live in a developing country and become part of that culture. That will help me get my bearings before I get caught up in the rush-rush corporate structure."

I was relieved to hear that even though the things the Vogts did to promote compassion in their children irked them at the time, they seem to be paying off now. Heidi comments, "My parents talked about starving people in Ethiopia all the time. We groaned about that stuff—that frustrated my parents. It was important that they tried. It had an impact later in life even if I wasn't paying attention too much at the time."

You *can* expect your kids to gripe and think you have "weird" values, but you also get to sit back and watch them eventually behave a little differently than the world around them.

What If They Get Discouraged?

This is a good question, because there are so many situations that are hopeless. For years I bought bags of oranges for Ethel, our "bag lady" friend, only to discover she gave them away. Her teeth were bad and she liked junk food better. I hardly knew how to tell my kids. The tendency to beat myself up (I'm not savvy—no teeth?) or judge the person being served (junk food!) was enormous.

Suppose you and your children are part of a tutoring program, but the other tutors rarely show up. Self-righteousness beckons: We're doing the right things while others are goofing off. It is important for the parent to be there for the child and to guard against burnout. One way to maintain a good perspective is to avoid sentimentality and idealism.

Teen volunteers, especially, are prone to idealism. They think the people in charge are saints, or that those poor people just need a break. They're missing reality: The people in charge make enormous mistakes; some of those poor people have had breaks and don't want your help, thank you. Volunteers in certain settings even get yelled at. Being an idealist is dangerous. When we see ourselves as do-gooders, we lose the opportunity for relationships and true reciprocity with the poor.

When you talk to kids, be realistic. If they're working in a soup kitchen with you, it's appropriate for them to know that a fair percentage of the people they serve are convicted felons, and another large percentage are otherwise nice people who happen to take a lot of drugs.

On the other hand, help your kids recognize when they encounter Christ in the middle of such service—and it will happen. A volunteer, who is otherwise quite normal, will donate a car or an apartment. A businessperson will hire some guys with all the wrong references.

Compassionate service to others becomes one more way we as parents and grandparents participate in the "saving" of our children's lives.

A so-called "needy" person will take pity on someone else and give away her dinner, her car, or—oh no!—the new, warm, thick socks you bought her!

Yes, we get discouraged, but God nurtures us through prayer and quiet worship. This is why prayer is important to those living out the compassion of Jesus Christ. The inward journey of prayer and the outward journey of service come together. Prayer can push away our do-gooder, fix-it, pushy tendencies. Service at its best flows from our companionship with God.

In the moments of disappointment and agony—a missionary is martyred, a homeless friend dies—it's OK to be transparent, even if that means whining and railing at God, who loves us indescribably. It's OK to teach our children to pray these angry psalms: "Why do the wicked renounce God and say in their hearts, 'You will not call us to account?'" and "Rise up O Lord; O God, lift up your hand; do not forget the oppressed" (Ps. 10:13, 12). As we're honest with God, God meets us.

Be Prepared to Change

You will become different. Some of your friends may wrinkle their forehead at the things you like to do and the "odd" people you spend time with. Compassionate encounters change you forever.

What You Can Expect to Happen

In Robert Coles's book *The Call of Service,* a nine-year-old talks about the changes she saw in her mother. The girl's sister had been diagnosed with acute leukemia. During the treatments, her mother overheard another child saying "how hard it was for her and her mother to get to the hospital for her chemotherapy treatments. With no car, they had to take a bus, then a subway, then switch to another bus. They arrived tired and often late for the dreaded treatments. In their shared jeopardy and apprehension, the two mothers got to talking, discussing their daughters' experiences."

This nine-year-old from an affluent, white family watched her mother become good friends with an African-American woman from a ghetto neighborhood. Her mother began giving the mother and child rides to treatments. Said the nine-year-old, "My mom has become a little different. She has been going to church a lot, and she doesn't worry about the usual stuff—what we eat and whether she's overspent on her allowance. She goes all the way to Roxbury to help that family; they've become her friends. . . .My mom is easier to live with. She's lost her [bad] temper! She's calm about everything, it seems!

"She drives them to the hospital and she waits, and then she drives them back. She says she talks with them better than [with] anyone. Daddy is scared because of the neighborhood, but Mom says the people are very nice to her. She says they're nicer than our neighbors, because the people in this town are always minding their own business. . . . Over there, people . . . stop you on the street and ask you how you're doing, and they seem to mean it."

Coles noted, "It is hard to decide which of the women offered more to the other. The well-to-do white suburban mother went out of her way to offer a service to the black mother: many days of driving in and out of the city. But the black mother extended her own service to these newfound friends of hers—prayers, occasional dishes prepared, and most of all, an attitude best described by the white mother: 'It was two miracles: our daughter getting better and meeting those people and going to their home. Every time she tells me how good I've been to her, I get all teary, and I tell her she's been a tremendous gift to us!'" What did the black mother learn? "'There are white folks who *care*, there really are,' confronting an incredulity earned through the grim lessons of a lifetime."[1]

Perhaps these positive effects of compassionate service are one of the many meanings of Jesus' statement that "those who want to save their life will lose it, and those who lose their life for my sake will find it" (Matt. 16:25). Compassionate service to others becomes one more way we as parents and grandparents participate in the "saving" of our children's lives. It also trains our kids to be the people we long for them to be—adults who work hard, who build loving relationships, who know and experience God. Defying the self-absorbed culture, they serve alongside us and let God's love shape them into compassionate people.

QUESTIONS FOR CONSIDERATION

Choose a few of the following questions to discuss with others or to ponder yourself.

1. What was most interesting to you in Heidi's remarks about growing up in a "different" home?
2. Which of these pitfalls are you most likely to experience? Why?
   ❑ being self-righteous
   ❑ being unrealistic
   ❑ not recognizing the moments when people portray Christ to you
3. How is reciprocity lived out in Robert Coles's story about the two mothers?

If you're planning to do a service project together for the next session, review chapters 11 and 13 for ideas about how to make it go well. Be sure to compliment others' children—an encouraging word from another adult means a lot, especially if their parents hear it too!

What You Can Expect to Happen

Personal Devotions

Read Matthew 25:31-45. Think of someone you've previously discounted. Imagine yourself serving that person and that person saying to you the words of verses 34-36.

PRAYER. With your transforming power, you, O God, can help me see you in people that I ignore. Give me that humble heart of Christ to recognize Christ in those I serve—even in the faces of these children I love. Amen.

Family Devotions

Ask your family to turn to Matthew 25:31-45. Assign parts to read aloud: king—verses 34-36, 40-43, 45; those on the right—verses 37-39; those on the left, verse 44. Act as narrator, reading all other verses. Tell about your meditation above.

PRAYER. Give us, O God, the eyes of those on the right. Help us to see you in the faces of those we tend to ignore and neglect. Help us to enjoy finding you in the people we serve. Amen.

Notes

Chapter 1

1. Interdenominational Foreign Mission Association, *Catch the Vision!* (brochure for IFMA Frontier Peoples Committee), 1990, second panel.
2. Henri J. M. Nouwen, *Making All Things New* (San Francisco: HarperSanFrancisco, 1981), 66.
3. Deborah Spaide, *Teaching Your Kids to Care: How to Discover and Develop the Spirit of Charity in Your Children* (Secaucus, N.J.: Citadel Press, 1995), 23.
4. Ibid., 15.
5. Jim Wallis, *The Soul of Politics* (New York: The New Press; Maryknoll, N.Y.: Orbis Books, 1994), 61.
6. Paul Borthwick, "What Can I Do for a Hungry World?" *Discipleship Journal* 96 (1996): 29.

Chapter 2

1. I am using this meaning of *culture:* "Culture is seen in what people do unthinkingly, what is 'natural' to them and therefore requires no explanation and justification." Dallas Willard, *The Divine Conspiracy* (San Francisco: HarperSanFrancisco, 1998), 260.
2. John Naisbitt, *Megatrends* (New York: Warner Books, 1984), 110; and John Naisbitt and Patricia Aburdene, *Megatrends 2000* (New York: Avon Books, 1990), xviii.
3. James McGinnis, "Households of Faith," *Weavings* 14, no. 5 (1999): 32.
4. Wallis, *The Soul of Politics*, 141.
5. Judith Smith, "Stewards in the Household of God," *Weavings* 14, no. 5 (1999): 10.
6. Deborah Spaide, *Teaching Your Kids to Care*, 13.
7. Patricia Depew, "Petition for Promising Breakthroughs," *Global Prayer Digest* 13, no. 10 (1994): Day 11.
8. Franklin Graham with Jeanette Lockerbie, *Bob Pierce: This One Thing I Do* (Waco, Tex.: Word Books, 1983), 77.

Chapter 3

1. *Alternative Gifts International* 14, no. 1 (1999): 1.
2. Joan Chittister, *Wisdom Distilled from the Daily* (San Francisco: HarperSanFrancisco, 1991), 126.
3. *Skate Attack* (brochure on Australian youth event, May 21–29), produced by Open Doors Australia, 7.
4. Louis Evely, *That Man Is You*, trans. by Edmond Bonin (Ramsey, N.J.: Paulist Press, 1964), 188, 179.
5. James B. McGinnis and Kathleen McGinnis, *Parenting for Peace and Justice: Ten Years Later* (Maryknoll, N.Y.: Orbis Books, 1990), 107.
6. John Robb with Larry Wilson, "Prayer Is Social Action," *World Vision* (February–March 1997): 4.

Chapter 4

1. Douglas K. Huneke, *The Moses of Rovno* (Tiburon, Calif.: Compassion House, 1985), 178–85.
2. Ibid., 180.
3. Ibid.
4. Ibid., 181.
5. Peter Benson, *All Kids Are Our Kids* (San Francisco: Jossey-Bass Publishers, 1997), 49.
6. Henri J. M. Nouwen, *Reaching Out* (New York: Doubleday, Image Book, 1975), 66–67.

Chapter 5

1. Spaide, *Teaching Your Kids to Care*, 3.
2. From "Promoting a New Standard of Excellence in Missions Education Resources," at http://www.21stcenturykidsconnect.org/resources.htm.
3. James McGinnis, *Educating for Peace and Justice: Religious Dimensions, K–6* (St. Louis, Mo.: Institute for Peace and Justice, 1993), 61.
4. May Sarton, Introduction to *The Russia House*, by John LeCarré (New York: Alfred A. Knopf, 1989), as quoted in Wallis, *The Soul of Politics*, 140.
5. Attributed to David Redding but not footnoted in Michael Shannon, *Lighten Up!* (Cincinnati, Ohio: Standard Publishing, 1999), 67.
6. *Causes of Hunger,* 1995 (Silver Springs, Md.: Bread for the World Institute, 1995), 107–8.

Chapter 6

1. The original version of this essay appeared in *Parenting for Peace and Justice Newsletter* 69 (September 1995): 3. Heidi has revised it, and I have shortened it.
2. Wallis, *The Soul of Politics,* 71.

Chapter 7

1. From "Nazi No More," at http://channel2000.com/news/specialassign/news specialassignment-981022-182754.html.
2. From "Rwandan Diary," The Compassion Project (Colorado Springs, Colo.: Compassion International, 1999). Video.
3. Dave Geisler, "Petition for Promising Breakthroughs," in *Global Prayer Digest* (July 1996): Day One.
4. Richard Saul Wurman, *Information Anxiety* (New York: Doubleday, 1989), 32.

Chapter 8

1. "10 Tips to Get Your Kids Excited about Missions" (Sierra Madre, Calif.: The Mission Vision Network), Tip 3. Brochure.
2. Janice Mall, "Plight of Homeless Families in Los Angeles," *Los Angeles Times,* 23 November 1986, Part VI, pp. 6–7 (based on a study done by sociologist Kay Young

McChesney of the University of Southern California Homeless Families Project).

Chapter 9
1. Kevin Johnson, *Catch the Wave* (Minneapolis, Minn.: Bethany House Publishers, 1996), 136.
2. Ed Welsh, *52 Fun Things Your Family Can Do Together for Missions*, revised (Pasadena, Calif.: Children's Mission Resource Center, 1994), 11.
3. Dan Harrison with Gordon Aeschliman, "Going Global," *Discipleship Journal* 96 (1996): 100.
4. Ibid.

Chapter 10
1. Bread for the World International, *At the Crossroads: The Future of Foreign Aid* (Silver Spring, Md.: BFWI, 1995), 18–19, quoted in Ronald J. Sider, *Rich Christians in an Age of Hunger* (Dallas, Tex.: Word Publishing, 1997), 259, 325.
2. Paul Borthwick, "What Can I Do for a Hungry World?" *Discipleship Journal* 96 (1996): 32.
3. For more information, go to this Web site: http://www.gn.apc.org/babymilk.
4. McGinnis and McGinnis, *Parenting for Peace and Justice: Ten Years Later*, 56.
5. John Baillie, *A Diary of Private Prayer* (London: Oxford University Press, 1936), 95.
6. Phil Bogosian, "Let the *Global Prayer Digest* Give Your Family a Heart for the World" (Pasadena, Calif.: Phil Bogosian).

Chapter 11
1. *Family Matters: The First Year* (Washington, D.C.: Points of Light Foundation/ W. K. Kellogg Foundation, 1992), 38–60.
2. "Think About It" (Colorado Springs, Colo.: International Students, Inc., 1997). Brochure.
3. H. L. Richard, "Some Pointers for Personal Evangelism among Educated Hindus," *Evangelical Missions Quarterly* 30 (April 1994): no. 2, reprinted in *Mission Frontiers Bulletin* (Sept.–Oct. 1996): 17.
4. James McGinnis, "Guidelines for Empowering Families to Service" (St. Louis, Mo.: Institute for Peace and Justice), no. 5.
5. Several of these ideas are adapted from the excellent handout "Guidelines for Empowering Families to Service," by James McGinnis (St. Louis, Mo.: Institute for Peace and Justice).

Chapter 12
1. The Louis Harris Associates, "Attitudes toward Racial and Religious Minorities and toward Women" (New York: National Conference of Christians and Jews, 1979), cited in Huneke, *The Moses of Rovno*, 184.
2. Huneke, *The Moses of Rovno,* 183.

3. Borthwick, *A Mind for Missions,* 91.
4. Dale Painter, "Extra-Value Vacations," *Discipleship Journal* 97 (1997): 32–33.

Chapter 13
1. Huneke, *The Moses of Rovno,* 184.
2. Welsh, *52 Fun Things Your Family Can Do Together for Missions,* 12.
3. Ibid., 1.
4. Ibid., 3.

Chapter 15
1. Borthwick, *A Mind for Missions,* 85–86.
2. Huneke, *The Moses of Rovno,* 184.
3. Paul Hiebert, "Culture and Cross-cultural Differences," *Perspectives on the World Christian Movement,* ed. Ralph D. Winter and Steven C. Hawthorne (Pasadena, Calif.: William Carey Library, 1981), 373–75.
4. Ruben Rumbaut, "The Challenge of Pluralism: Old Minorities and New Immigrants" (remarks made at a conference titled "What's Next? American Pluralism and the Civic Culture," November 1999 at Smith College, Northampton, Mass.)

Chapter 16
1. Tony Campolo, *Wake Up America: Answering God's Radical Call While Living in the Real World* (San Francisco: HarperSanFrancisco, 1991), 7.
2. May Sarton, as quoted in Wallis, *The Soul of Politics,* 140.
3. From "Radio Spot," at http://www.adbusters.org/toolbox/radio.htm. (For more information, call 800-663-1243.)
4. Susan Vogt, "Children, Money and Values: Ten Principles," *Parenting for Peace & Justice Newsletter* 65 (December 1994): 1, 6.

Chapter 17
1. Robert Coles, *The Call of Service* (Boston, Mass.: Houghton Mifflin, 1993), 48–50.

Resources

In this book, I've referred to various organizations that can help you. Here I offer a list of the following: organizations and events, books (for children, teens, and parents), videos, magazines, resources for children and youth workers, and catalogs of gifts that help others.

Organizations and Events

Alternatives for Simple Living. 5312 Morningside Ave., P.O. Box 2787, Sioux City, Iowa 51106, 800-821-6153, http://www.SimpleLiving.org. Resources for responsible living and celebrating, including videos, books, stories to read aloud, booklets, gift ideas, activity books for kids, activity and discussion guides, games, family night activity books, music, publications—all focusing on simplifying holidays, simplicity, peace and justice, anticonsumerism.

Boycotts In Action/Co-Op America (Publisher of *National Green Pages*™). 1612 K Street NW, Suite 600, Washington, DC 20006, 800-58-GREEN, http://www.coopamerica.org/boycotts/bantargetchart.htm. Provides information on current boycotts against corporations.

Children's Mission Resource Center. U.S. Center for World Mission, 1605 Elizabeth St., Pasadena, CA 91104, gerry.dueck@wciu.edu, http://www.uscwm.org. Supplies children's mission resources by mail, E-mail, and in person through Mission Resource Center bookstore. Carries over 150 different titles of children's items, including curricula, story books, videos, and visual-aids.

Church World Service. P.O. Box 968, Elkhart, IN 46514-0968, 800-297-1516, http://www.ChurchWorldService.org. Thirty-five Protestant, Anglican, and Orthodox faith communions join together in partnership through Church World Service. They cooperate worldwide in programs of long-term development, emergency response to disasters, and assistance to refugees. Children and families can easily join the effort by preparing school kits, health kits, cleaning or sewing kits, or layettes. CWS also has a blanket distribution program and sponsors crop walks.

Compassion International. P.O. Box 7000, Colorado Springs, CO 80933, 800-336-7676, http://www.compassion.com. A Christian child-sponsoring organization focusing on child development. Offers curriculum for teens.

Evangelicals for Social Action. 10 East Lancaster Ave., Wynnewood, PA 19096-3495, 800-650-6600, http://www.esa-online.org. An organization that challenges and equips Christians to be agents of God's redemption and transformation in the world through reflection on church and society; training in holistic ministry; linking people together for mutual learning and action. Helps Christians consider their commitment to the world in light of their commitment to Christ.

Habitat for Humanity. 121 Habitat St., Americus, GA 31709, 800-HABITAT, http://www.habitat.org. Helps people who need affordable housing build their own homes with "sweat equity." Uses volunteers, sometimes families. Look in your phone book for local chapters.

Heifer Project International. P.O. Box 8058, Little Rock, AR 72203, 800-422-0474, http://www.heifer.org. Gifts of animals and training in the care of the animals help hungry families around the world feed themselves and become self-reliant. Children love giving chickens, goats, bees, and more to other children who are hungry.

International Students, Inc. P.O. Box C, Colorado Springs, CO 80901, 800-ISI-TEAM, E-mail: information@isionline.org, http://www.isionline.org. Provides statistics and information about befriending international students.

National Charities Information Bureau. 19 Union Square West, New York, NY 10003, http://www.give.org. A charity watchdog organization that evaluates charities and offers a free Wise Giving Guide of national charities.

National Coalition for the Homeless. 1012 Fourteenth Street, NW, Suite #600, Washington, DC 20005-3406, http://www.nch.ari.net. A national advocacy network of homeless persons, activists, service providers, and others committed to ending homelessness through public education, policy advocacy, grassroots organizing, and technical assistance. The Web site provides several directories if you're looking for a place to volunteer (for example, Directory of National Homeless and Housing Organizations, Directory of Local Homeless Service Organizations, Directory of State Contacts for the Education of Homeless Children and Youth).

The Other Side. 300 W. Apsley St., Philadelphia, PA 19144, http://www.the otherside.org. A Christian ministry with a vision for social transformation that takes seriously both personal spirituality and the struggle for social and economic justice. While the primary ministry is its magazine, The Other Side also offers study guides, Web-site ministry, an alternative seminary, ecumenical dialogue, and prisoner correspondence program.

Parenting for Peace and Justice Network. Institute for Peace and Justice, 4144 Lindell Blvd. #408, St. Louis, MO 63108, http://www.ipj-ppj.org. An interfaith, interracial, transnational association of families of all descriptions who seek "shalom"—well-being, wholeness, peace, justice—in our own living situations and in the broader community. Offers a newsletter, discounts on PPJN resources, leadership mailings, enrichment workshops, and local and family support groups.

Samaritan's Purse. P.O. Box 3000, Boone, NC 28607, http://www.samaritans purse.org. A relief and development organization. Offers a Christmas gift catalog.

Sojourners. 2401 15th St. NW, Washington, DC 20009, http://www.sojourn ers.com. A grassroots network for personal, community, and political transformation, rooted in the prophetic biblical tradition. Offers old truths and new visions for changing times, beyond both the religious right and the secular left, combining personal faith and social justice, prayer with peacemaking, spirituality with politics. Offers a magazine and a community in Washington, DC.

Teaching Tolerance. 400 Washington Ave., Montgomery, AL 36104. http://splcenter.org. A project of the Southern Poverty Law Center offering a magazine, posters, videos, and kits focusing on tolerance for school teachers and organizations.

21st Century Kids Connect. PMB 205, 7109 Staples Mill Road, Richmond, VA 23228-4110, 800-206-9431, http://www.21stcenturykidsconnect.org. A team of experts dedicated to enhancing children's mission education by networking, research, resources, resource evaluation, and training. The International Children's Expo helps children's workers build their vision and equips them with methods and tools to lead children. Sponsors mission trips through King's Kids International, which encourages discipleship of children and teens in context of outreach and missions. Teams are for children ages six through eighteen. A parent must accompany a child ten or under. On most trips, entire families are welcome, even with children under age six.

United Methodist Children's Fund for Christian Mission. P.O. Box 340013, Nashville, TN 37203-0013. Children can learn about specific mission projects through information packets with activity ideas, then choose projects to support through contributions.

Urbana-Student Missions Convention. P.O. Box 7895, Madison, WI 53707-7895, http://www.urbana.org. A triennial student missions convention drawing more than seventeen thousand students to the University of Illinois at Urbana-Champaign for learning, worship, prayer, and discussion about missions and evangelism. Sponsored by InterVarsity Christian Fellowship to help students explore short-term and career opportunities in missions.

World Relief. P.O. Box WRC, Dept. 800, Wheaton, IL 60189, 800-535-5433, http://www.worldrelief.org. A Christian relief and development organization that partners with churches and missions of National Association of Evangelicals. Offers a holiday gift program and curriculum for children.

World Vision. 34834 Weyerhauser Way S., Federal Way, WA 98001, 800-448-6437, http://www.worldvision.org. An international relief and development company with a magazine, a large child-sponsorship program, and holiday gift catalog.

Books

Books for Children and Teens

Coles, Robert. *The Story of Ruby Bridges.* New York: Scholastic, 1995. For ages 4–8. This is a moving story of six-year-old Ruby's incredible courage and forgiveness during the integration of a New Orleans elementary school.

Ferrell, Frank, and Janet Ferrell. *Trevor's Place: The Story of the Boy Who Brings Hope to the Homeless.* Gladwyne, Penn.: Trevor's Endeavors (only available from the authors, P.O. Box 21, Gladwyne, PA 19035).

Flegal, Daphna. *Sign and Say: Bible Verses for Children.* Nashville, Tenn.: Abingdon, 1999. Children ages 3–12 can learn favorite Bible verses, both Old and New Testament, in American Sign Language.

Hibschman, Barbara. *I Want to Be a Missionary.* Camp Hill, Penn.: Christian Publications, 1990. For grades 1–6. A twenty-four–page book that allows children to dream about being a missionary with a specific assignment described in a Go, Show, and Tell format: teachers, evangelists, Bible translators, doctors and nurses, pilots, radio and television personnel, relief workers, etc. Also available in Spanish.

———. *Please Leave Your Shoes at the Door.* Camp Hill, Penn.: Christian Publications, 1992. Part of the Jaffray Collection of Missionary Portraits with versions written specifically for children. Stories of snakes, accidents, war, and dangerous travel adventures that include a ride on an elephant. Young readers (ages 4–7) learn of God's faithfulness through the lives of missionaries to Thailand, Elmer and Corrine Sahlberg.

Lewis, Barbara A. *The Kid's Guide to Service Projects: Over 500 Service Ideas for Young People Who Want to Make a Difference.* Minneapolis, Minn.: Free Spirit Publishing, 1995. For ages 9–12. Something for everyone who wants to make a difference, from simple projects to large-scale commitments. Kids can choose from a variety of topics, including animals, crime fighting, the environment, friendship, hunger, literacy, politics and government, and transformation.

Myers, Bill. *My Life as Crocodile Junk Food.* Nashville, Tenn.: Tommy Nelson, 1993. For ages 8–12. One title in Bill's witty Incredible Worlds of Wally McDoogle series. Thirteen-year-old Wally visits a missionary friend in South America and in his typical style of madcap misadventure learns the importance of the work they do.

Roehlkepartain, Jolene L. *Teaching Kids to Care & Share: 300+ Mission & Service Ideas for Children.* Nashville, Tenn.: Abingdon, 2000. Hands-on activities involve children in service to one another, their churches, and local communities, and the world.

Books for Teens

Benson, Peter L., and Eugene C. Roehlkepartain. *Beyond Leaf Raking: Learning to Serve/Serving to Learn.* Nashville, Tenn.: Abingdon, 1993. Inspires youth with stories from congregations that have effectively involved youth in service. Provides checklists, worksheets, and guidelines for evaluation and sharing.

Bushor, Mark. *Mission Mania: Crazy to Serve.* Nashville, Tenn.: Abingdon, 2000. Teens' own stories about making a difference in the world because of their decision to be disciples of Jesus Christ inspire youth and encourage teenagers to share their stories with peers. Offers practical guidance on serving others. A Leader's Guide, *Mission Mania: A Can-Do Guide for Youth,* provides five lessons and suggestions for go-and-do learning beyond church walls.

Duper, Linda Leeb. *160 Ways to Help the World: Community Service Projects for Young People.* New York: Facts on File, 1996. For young adult readers. Gives step-by-step directions for organizing kids for service, especially through a church, school, or community organization.

Johnson, Kevin. *Catch the Wave! Grabbing Your Chance to Change the World.* Minneapolis, Minn.: Bethany House Publishers, 1996. An upbeat manual that persuades and instructs teens on how to "grab your chance to change the world" in missions and service projects. Get more information about mission trips from Kevin at his Web site: http://www.thewave.org.

Servant Journal. Nashville, Tenn.: Cokesbury, 1996. For youth to record their personal reflections on an experience of serving others. Includes devotional thoughts. It is pocket-sized, adaptable for five to ten days.

Books for Parents

Borthwick, Paul. *A Mind for Missions: Ten Ways to Build Your World Vision.* Colorado Springs, Colo.: NavPress, 1987. This excellent book provides practical ideas and great stories without making you feel like a doofus for not caring more about missions.

Gill, Athol. *Life on the Road: The Gospel Basis for a Messianic Lifestyle.* Scottdale, Penn.: Herald Press, 1992. How the life of Jesus is related to life today, countering popular teaching of comfortable Christianity.

González, Justo. *When Christ Lives in Us.* Nashville, Tenn: Abingdon, 1996. An adult study that explores how today's adult Christians may walk with Jesus in specific forms and acts of ministry.

Howell, James. *Yours Are the Hands of Christ.* Nashville, Tenn.: Upper Room Books, 1998. A call to renewed commitment to faithful discipleship and practice of our Christian faith.

Ives, Jane. *Transforming Ventures: A Spiritual Guide for Volunteers in Mission.* Nashville, Tenn.: Upper Room Books, 2000. Explores eight themes for spiritual growth before, during, and after a mission experience.

Kraybill, Donald. *The Upside Down Kingdom.* Scottdale, Penn.: Herald Press, 1979. Disciples of Jesus favor those suffering at society's margins. This book helps those who doubt the biblical support for a "socialized gospel" and new believers who have "walked the sawdust trail" and wonder, What now?

McGinnis, James B., and Kathleen McGinnis. *Parenting for Peace and Justice: Ten Years Later.* Maryknoll, N.Y.: Orbis Books, 1990. How one family has taught their children about family social action, family prayer, racial attitudes, and consumerism. (May be ordered from the Parenting for Peace and Justice Network listed above.)

Ogbonnoya, A. Okechukwu. *Missionaries.* Nashville, Tenn.: Abingdon, 1996. Part of a series, Bible People, this book offers information about Barnabas, Jonah, Timothy, Onesimus, Lydia, Peter, Priscilla and Aquila.

Pickens-Jones, Linda L. *Strangers into Friends: Hospitality as Mission.* Nashville, Tenn.: Abingdon, 2000. A five-session study for adults which delves into the biblical concept of hospitality. Encourages participants to expamine if, how, and when they can extend themselves for others.

Sine, Tom. *Live It Up! How to Create a Life You Can Love.* Scottdale, Penn.: Herald Press, 1994. Offers new and biblical ways to move away from the stress-track and take up God's offer of a festive, satisfying life.

Spaide, Deborah. *Teaching Your Kids to Care: How to Discover and Develop the Spirit of Charity in Your Children:* Secaucus, N.J.: Citadel Press, 1995. An excellent down-to-earth book with 105 ideas of ways kids can serve others.

UMY Mission and Event Annual: Workshops, Retreats, & Mission Ideas for Youth. Nashville, Tenn.: Cokesbury, 1996. Ideas for planning longer events, such as retreats, all-day mission programs, or a series of workshops.

Vogt, Susan, ed. *Just Family Nights: Sixty Activities to Keep Your Family Together in a World Falling Apart.* Elgin, Ill.: Brethren Press, 1994. Includes sixty family-night formats for families or small groups and applies to a broad cross-section of ethnic, racial, and religious backgrounds. Themes include such topics as Videos and Values. (May be ordered from the Parenting for Peace and Justice Network listed above.)

Welsh, Ed. *52 Fun Things Your Family Can Do Together for Missions* (booklet, revised edition). Pasadena, Calif.: Children's Mission Resource Center, 1994. Practical fun ideas for activities to do with your kids.

Videos

The following organizations rent and sell videos with compassion-related themes.

Alternatives for Simple Living. *See* Organizations above.

Church World Service/Film Library Resources for Global Education, P.O.

Box 968, Elkhart, IN 46515-0968, 800-297-1516, http://www.church worldservice.org. A ministry of the World Council of Churches. Films, videos, slide shows, and filmstrips; available on a free loan basis to churches, schools, and community organizations. Resources on hunger and development issues, the environment, war and peacemaking, refugees, human rights. Also stories of people, "Faith in Action," and special videos for children and youth.

Mennonite Central Committee, Resource Catalog, U.S. Resource Library, 21 S. 12th St., P.O. Box 500, Akron, PA 17501-0500, http://www.mcc.org. Videos, films, periodicals, posters, brochures, flyers, booklets, exhibits. Child's View Series" shows how children in different parts of the world live. Other videos are about justice, food and malnutrition, environment, peace and militarism, racial reconciliation, social awareness, and specific parts of the world. Several videos address "affluenza," examine living a simpler life, complete with "anti-commercials." All videos are available for free loan for a month; the only cost is return shipping. Some are available for purchase, or purchase information can be acquired.

Individual Videos

The following videos are available to rent from many sources or in some cases from libraries. You can watch them and discuss them with your kids. Some, of course, are only appropriate for teens.

Alan and Naomi (PG, 1992) portrays the friendship between a young survivor of the Holocaust and a Christian peer in New York City.

Amazing Grace and Chuck (PG, 1987) is about a young baseball player who sparks an international effort to dismantle nuclear missiles.

Cry Freedom (PG, 1987) shows the short life of South African activist Steven Biko and his friendship with white news editor Donald Woods.

Dead Man Walking (R, 1995) is about the power of compassion rather than capital punishment to deal with violent crime.

El Norte (R, 1983) shows how two Guatemalan teens (brother and sister) sneak across the U.S. border to escape political persecution and the threat of death.

Elephant Man (PG, 1980) deals with societal violence against those who are different.

RESOURCES

Entertaining Angels: The Dorothy Day Story (Paulist Press) features the life of a woman who gave herself to God and to the poor and founded the Catholic Worker Movement in New York.

The Fisher King (R, 1991) explores the life of a homeless person, what can drive a person to such despair, yet how a homeless person can give to others.

Gandhi (PG, 1982) is the inspiring biography of India's great spiritual leader and nonviolence advocate.

Heaven Can Wait (PG, 1978). A football player, taken to heaven before his time, returns to earth. He takes over the body of a corrupt businessman and tries to change business tactics so that caring for people is important.

Karate Kid II (PG, 1986) illustrates using compassion rather than fists to overcome hostility.

Long Walk Home (PG, 1989) is a fictional version of the Montgomery, Alabama, bus boycott.

Norma Rae (PG, 1979), *Silkwood* (R, 1983), and *Marie* (PG-13, 1985) each celebrate a woman challenging injustice in the workplace.

The Power of One (PG-13, 1992) focuses on a youth doing the "right thing" to confront violence in South Africa.

Romero (1989) is the story of the assassinated Archbishop of San Salvador who championed the poor.

Sarafina! (PG-13, 1992). Set in Soweto, South Africa, this musical-political story portrays a young girl's coming of age.

Schindler's List (R, 1993) is the story of a man whose actions saved over one thousand Jews during the Holocaust.

Swing Kids (PG-13, 1993) shows teens making moral choices about joining the Hitler Youth Movement.

The War (PG-13, 1994) is a touching story for all ages on family, neighborhood, and global conflict and reconciliation.

Trevor's Endeavors. This ten-minute video can be ordered from Frank and Janet Ferrell, P.O. Box 21 Gladwyne, PA 19035.

Magazines

Global Prayer Digest, published by the U.S. Center for World Mission, 1605 Elizabeth St., Pasadena, CA 91104.

New World Outlook, published bimonthly by the General Board of Global Ministries of The United Methodist Church. For subscription information: Service Center, 7820 Reading Road, Cincinnati, OH 45222-1800. Reports for U.S. and more than 130 countries where United Methodists are in mission.

The Other Side. See Organizations above.

Prism. Published by Evangelicals for Social Action (*see* Organizations above).

Sojourners. See Organizations above.

World Christian. Published quarterly by World in Need, Inc., P.O. Box 1357, Oak Park, IL 60304, 888-524-5070, WINpress7@aol.com. Viewing world news with the eyes of God's worldwide purposes.

World Vision. See Organizations above.

Resources for Children and Youth Workers

The All-Purpose Youth Service Kit: Youth Serving with Jesus. Nashville, Tenn.: Cokesbury (800-672-1789). Five sessions provide ideas that have proven effective for groups preparing for mission projects. May be used in conjunction with *Servant Journal* (*see* Books for Teens above).

Burns, Jim, and Mike DeVries. *Missions and Service Projects: Fresh Ideas.* Ventura, Calif.: Gospel Light Publications (805-644-9721). Dozens of group-tested ideas for meaningful mission ventures for junior and senior high groups.

The Compassion Project. Compassion International, http://www.compassion project.com. *See* Compassion International under Organizations above. A five-session program available free. Includes videos, games, and other activities designed to teach youth about poverty and how to respond to it. Targeted to young people ages 13–17.

In My Own Words. Colorado Springs: Colo.: Compassion International (800-336-7676). Three sessions for junior-high kids. Includes video and workbook.

RESOURCES

Kids on a Mission. Colorado Springs, Colo.: The Christian and Missionary Alliance CE Ministries Office (http://www.cmalliance.org). Curriculum for grades 1–5 that teaches children about unreached people and the Great Commission. It includes seven units, each with a video segment and reproducible student sheets and activities.

McGinnis, James B. and Dolores Kirk. *Educating for Peace and Justice: Religious Dimensions, K–6.* St. Louis, Mo.: Institute for Peace and Justice (may be ordered from the Parenting for Peace and Justice Network; *see* Organizations above). A ninety-six–page manual with music, games, art and craft activities on peacemaking, nonviolence, global interdependence, interracial reconciliation.

Neufeld, Christine. *Peace: Just Live It.* Newton, Kans.: Faith & Light Press (316-283-5100). Ten studies on being a peaceful person and participating in social justice projects.

Passport to Hope. Wheaton, Ill.: World Relief (800-535-5433). Six sessions (for third- to sixth-graders, roughly) with activity sheets and video. Includes viewing a child from each of several countries, Nicaragua, Bangladesh, Mozambique, Cambodia, and Rwanda.

Shearer, Jody Miller. *Living without Violence.* Newton, Kans.: Faith & Light Press (316-283-5100). Five Bible studies for junior high kids on being peaceful, even with enemies and when angry.

UMY Mission Event Annual: Workshops, Retreats, & Mission Ideas for Youth. Nashville, Tenn.: Cokesbury (800-672-1789). Ideas for different types of events—retreats, all-day mission programs, or a series of workshops.

The Upper Room Web site. http://www.upperroom.org. At this Web site, see pages for *Devo'Zine*® and *Pockets*®. *Devo'Zine*® (for teens) and *Pockets*® (for six- to twelve-year-olds) are print magazines with companion Web pages, which include ideas for parents or adults who work with kids as well.

Youth Specialties. *Student Underground: An Event Curriculum on the Persecuted Church.* Grand Rapids, Mich.: Zondervan, 2000. Four sessions, including award-winning movie *Behind the Sun.* Ideal for lock-in weekend event.

Gifts

Alternative Gift Markets. P.O. Box 2267, Lucerne Valley, CA 92356, 800-842-2243, E-mail: altgifts@sisp.net, http://www.altgifts.org. Ideal for children giving you and others gifts all year around. Gifts as low as $5. Catalog has pictures; organization sends recipient beautiful card explaining gift.

Catalog of Hope. World Relief, P.O. Box WRC Dept. 80, Wheaton, IL 60189, 800-535-5433, http://www.worldrelief.org. Gifts begin as low as $1.25. Kids can go online with their allowance money for an exciting shopping experience that will make a lasting impression.

Global Gift Guide. World Concern, 19303 Fremont Avenue North; Seattle, WA 98133, 800-755-5022, E-mail: wconcern@crista.org, http://www.world concern.org. You can buy a family in the developing world their own goat or even a well.

Samaritan's Purse Holiday Gift Giving Catalog. Samaritan's Purse. Call 800-353-5957 during the holiday season to get a catalog; otherwise use contacts listed in Organizations above. Items such as hot meals for a week ($7) and livestock and farm projects ($40). Their Operation Christmas Child distributes gift-filled shoeboxes in sixty countries.

SERRV International: Gifts That Make a Difference. P.O. Box 365, 500 Main St., New Windsor, MD 21776-0365, 800-422-5915, E-mail: info@serrv.org, http://www.serrv.org. Crafts from around the world, secured through fair trade practices with the artisans, are offered for individuals to purchase. Churches and nonprofit organizations can order on consignment for special sales events.

Ten Thousand Villages. 704 Main Street, P.O. Box 500, Akron, PA 17501-0500, 800-592-7238, http://www.villages.com. Stores and catalogs feature crafts made by disadvantaged artisans from around the world. Gifts can be purchased year-round for holidays, weddings, and birthdays—any occasion. Check for location of retail stores on Web site. Churches and community organizations can also arrange a seasonal sales event featuring Ten Thousand Villages merchandise.

World Vision Christmas Gift Catalogs. World Vision (*see* Organizations above). Also, http://www.worldvisiongifts.org. Allows you to purchase gifts in the name of your loved ones that will go to a needy person, family, or village.

About the Author

Jan Johnson is a speaker, teacher, and writer. An award-winning author of fourteen books and over a thousand magazine articles, she explores subjects from fitness to recovery issues to spiritual formation. As a speaker at retreats and conferences, she seeks to ignite a burning desire to know God in an authentic way. She received a degree in Christian education and biblical studies from Ozark Christian College. Jan is married and has two children.

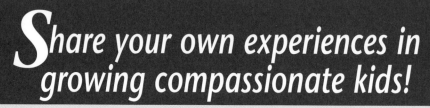

*S*hare your own experiences in growing compassionate kids!

Upper Room® Ministries invites you to describe briefly, on the reverse side of this page, ideas or activities that nurture compassion in kids and that have worked in your family. Your contribution may be shared with other families on The Upper Room® web site (**http://www.upperroom.org**) under the headings *Pockets*® or *Dēvo'Zine*®. *Pockets*® (for six- to twelve-year-olds) and *Dēvo'Zine*® (for teens) are print magazines with companion web pages. Both offer ideas for parents and adults who work with kids, and both invite input. Check them out!

P.S. If you would prefer to E-mail your stories, send them to **compassion@upperroom.org**.

FOLD, SECURE BOTTOM EDGE WITH TAPE, AND MAIL.

Growing Compassionate Kids

BUSINESS REPLY MAIL
FIRST-CLASS MAIL PERMIT NO. 1540 NASHVILLE TN
POSTAGE WILL BE PAID BY ADDRESSEE

UPPER
ROOM.
BOOKS

EDITORIAL
PO BOX 340004
NASHVILLE, TN 37203-9526

Please share your experiences here:

Name: (print) _____

Signature: _____
Your submission of this card and signature constitutes permission for use of the story in print or on the web at **www.upperroom.org**.

Please supply one or both ways to contact you:

Phone: _____ E-mail: _____

THANK YOU!

"This book guides parents, grandparents, and caregivers as they seek to he children grow as *disciples* of Christ—disciples who care about others and seek justice in the world. With specific examples, Jan Johnson opens for the reader a *new world* of possibilities where making a difference for others becom a way of life."
> —MARY ALICE GRAN
> Director, Children's Ministries
> General Board of Discipleship, The United Methodist Church

"A wonderful antidote to both 'compassion fatigue' and the frustrations of Christian parenting in a selfish society. Johnson's book offers practical ideas an valuable encouragement for reaching out."
> —RONALD J. SIDER
> President, Evangelicals for Social Action

"Jan Johnson gently nudges the heart of a mother, who imprints compassion in the hearts of her children. In this book, she tells us how to teach kids to care about others, which also teaches them about God. What greater legacy could w leave our children?"
> —CAROL KUYKENDALL
> Director of MOPS International (Mothers of Preschoolers)

"*Growing Compassionate Kids* is a wonderful blend of thoughtful teaching, compelling illustrations, and practical suggestions. It is a work that is very much needed in our present day Christian culture and, if implemented, can change the coming generation. I highly recommend it to all who are serious about spiritual formation."
> —MARTI ENSIGN
> Board Member, Renovaré

JAN JOHNSON is a speaker, teacher, and writer. An award-winning author of fourteen books and over a thousand magazine articles, she explores subjects from fitness to parenting to spiritual formation. As a popular speaker at retreats and conferences, she ignites a burning desire to know God in an authentic way. She received a degree in Christian education and biblical studies from Ozark Christian College. Jan is married and has two grown children.

ISBN 0-8358-0932-3

9 780835 809320   90000

UPPER
ROOM BOOK